M000304984

Nondenominational Judaism

Perspectives on Pluralism and Inclusion in
21st-Century
Jewish Professional Education

Edited by
Jonathan L. Friedmann,
Joel Gereboff,
and
Stephen Robbins

Ben Yehuda Press
Teaneck, New Jersey

NONDENOMINATIONAL JUDAISM: PERSPECTIVES ON PLURALISM AND INCLUSION IN 21ST-CENTURY JEWISH PROFESSIONAL EDUCATION ©2020 by the authors. All rights reserved. No part of this book may be used or reproduced in any manner whatsoever without written permission except in the case of brief quotations embodied in critical articles and reviews.

Published by Ben Yehuda Press
122 Ayers Court #1B
Teaneck, NJ 07666

http://www.BenYehudaPress.com

To subscribe to our monthly book club and support independent Jewish publishing, visit
https://www.patreon.com/BenYehudaPress

Ben Yehuda Press books may be purchased at a discount by synagogues, book clubs, and other institutions buying in bulk. For information, please email
markets@BenYehudaPress.com

ISBN13 978-1-953829-04-7

21 22 23 / 10 9 8 7 6 5 4 3 2 1   20210104

Contents

Teaching

Communities

Preface

The idea for this anthology was hatched at a faculty meeting of the Academy for Jewish Religion California (AJRCA) in January 2019. Coinciding with AJRCA's annual winter retreat at the Brandeis-Bardin campus in Simi Valley, California, the meeting was spent reflecting on the school's impending twentieth anniversary (2020) and how our ideas and implementations of "transdenominational Judaism" had evolved over the past two decades.

Prior to the meeting, faculty members received copies of "The 70 Faces of Torah," a *shiur* (study) on transdenominationalism presented by AJRCA co-founder Rabbi Stephen Robbins in 2005. The paper sparked three questions: What does "transdenominational Judaism" mean? Are we living up to that mission? What are the next steps for institutional engagement?

AJRCA recognizes that Judaism is not monolithic or fixed in time, but is an evolving and adapting system rooted in certain values and principles. AJRCA was founded on the ideal of gathering from the thought and practices of all Jewish movements and denominations. The Academy's mission is to draw from the entire corpus of Jewish law, literature, and experience, and to participate in an evolving and multifarious search for truth that blends past, present, and future insights without needing to uphold a particular denominational structure.

Minutes from the faculty meeting include a number of pithy statements. Combined, they form both a working definition of transdenominational Judaism and a guide for actualization:

1. There are 70 faces of Torah and each of us holds a piece of the whole;
2. Appreciating the essence(s) of Judaism over its form(s);
3. Nonjudgmental acceptance of Jews (and non-Jews) from different backgrounds;
4. Genuine curiosity about those whose ideas and practices differ from our own;
5. Embodying rather than teaching;
6. Honoring the diverse expressions of Jewish life;
7. Exposure to different types of communities, rituals, customs, and education.

These and other topics were too large for a single meeting or a single seminary. An invitation was sent to faculty, administrators, and alumni from AJRCA and other institutions engaged in pluralistic, nondenominational, and transdenominational Jewish professional and higher education. Participants were asked to share personal, academic, and/or philosophical reflections on their experiences learning, teaching, administrating, and leading in pluralistic Jewish settings; the unique roles of pluralism vis-à-vis denominational models; the benefits and challenges of nondenominational Jewish education; and related themes of their choosing.

This book anthologizes those responses. The eclectic understandings and approaches are a testament to the diversity and inclusivity of Judaism beyond denominational barriers, and, it is hoped, a contribution to larger conversations concerning changing attitudes and affiliations of twenty-first-century American Jews. It is our conviction that as conventional Jewish structures and institutions continue their gradual erosion, nondenominational approaches will help ensure a rich and viable future for American Judaism.

The editors are grateful to the authors for sharing their hearts and minds, and to Larry Yudelson, editorial director of Ben Yehuda Press, for his patience, enthusiasm, and confidence in this project.

Introduction

Jonathan L. Friedmann and Joel Gereboff

The experience of forming, joining, leaving, and witnessing the disappearance of institutions, organizations, and societies has been typical for Jews over the centuries. While affiliation with some such structure was compulsory in past phases of Jewish history, in the modern era—and especially in America—all Jewish affiliation is voluntary. Some institutions established by American Jews have endured for long periods. Such groups have sought to "police" their borders, demarcating clear and distinct identities via charters and statements of principles. But, given the reality of voluntary participation—as well as the diverse backgrounds and life experiences of American Jews— other organizations have sought out new frontiers and have created alternative models. These include the founding of training programs for Jewish clergy across or beyond the spectrum of affiliations.

Despite some earlier efforts to create rabbinic seminaries for all American Jews—not identified with any existing or emerging denomination or branch—by 1950, only denominationally affiliated seminaries existed. Shortly thereafter, a pluralistic Jewish seminary was founded in Yonkers, New York, which became the Academy for Jewish Religion. No other such institutions emerged until the turn of the twenty-first century. They, along with other developments, point to the diminishing role of denominational affiliation among American Jews, as well as efforts to work across denominational divides. Although some advocate for a post-denominational American Judaism, denominations persist in the form of synagogues, clergy and lay organizations, and seminaries. Pluralistic seminaries occupy a middle ground. Neither affirming nor seeking to eliminate denominational affiliation, they bring faculty and students together from a range of Jewish self-definitions to study, respond to growing trends in American Jewish life, and ultimately lead diverse institutions—some of which are explicitly denominational, some post-denominational, and some pluralistic.

In his recently published book, *The New American Judaism: How Jews Practice Their Religion Today*, Jack Wertheimer describes a number of efforts to establish nondenominational and post-denominational programs and institutions.[1] Following an examination of current challenges and tensions within the Orthodox, Conservative, and Reform movements, Wertheimer asks: "Who Needs Jewish Denominations?" In his analysis, denominational boundaries have become largely indistinct and porous in the "lives of ordinary Jews," who tend to favor personalism, volunteerism, and DIY-ism. These factors, which have affected American religion more broadly, were intensified in the Jewish community by denominational controversies during the latter twentieth century. In response, institutions have created forums for bringing Jews together, coalescing in the emergence of a "transdenominational culture." Wertheimer lists several examples, including Machon Hadar, an egalitarian educational center in New York City; the Jerusalem-based Hartman Institute, which has extensive programming in North America; the folding of various Jewish day school associations into one group (Prizma); and the founding of seminaries with the express purpose of drawing students from different sectors of the Jewish population.[2]

Whereas the denominations began as ideological movements, striving to define the "essence" of Jewish belief and practice through treatises, platforms, and mission statements, contemporary developments tend to be more pragmatic. Whether the approach is nondenominational (not affiliating with a particular denomination), transdenominational (drawing from all denominations), post-denominational (moving beyond denominations), interdenominational (collaborating between denominations), pluralistic (valuing different

---

[1] Jack Wertheimer, *The New American Judaism: How Jews Practice Their Religion Today* (Princeton, NJ: Princeton University Press, 2018). Several reviewers critique aspects of Wertheimer's work, especially in terms of his "essentialist" notion of Judaism. See, for example, Rebecca Alpert, *Journal of the American Academy of Religion* 87 (2019): 559–62, and Shaul Kelner, *Sociology of Religion* 80 (2019): 545–46.

[2] Ibid., 165. Jonathan Sarna, in his updated conclusion to his *American Judaism: A History* (New Haven, CT: Yale University Press, 2019), 385, also comments on the founding of pluralistic seminaries, which he attributes to the breakdown of authority of religious leaders.

approaches), inclusive (embracing all comers), some combination of these, or another label, they are each practical responses to the reality that denominational membership is no longer a given, and that an open Judaism—however defined—is an effective way of attracting the unaffiliated (or ambiguously affiliated) in an age of fragmentation and hyper-individualism.

Of course, denominations have not disappeared. According to Pew Research Center's 2013 study, "A Portrait of Jewish Americans," 35% of U.S. Jews self-identify as Reform, 18% as Conservative, 10% as Orthodox, and 6% as "other" (e.g., Reconstructionist, Renewal, Humanistic). However, the second highest affiliation is no affiliation at all: 30% of American Jews claim no denomination—including 19% of "Jews by religion" and two-thirds of "Jews of no religion," as defined by the study. Denominational switching is also commonplace, typically in the direction of less stringent forms: 25% of people raised Orthodox become Conservative or Reform; 30% of people raised Conservative become Reform; 28% of people raised Reform leave denominations altogether.[3]

Partly because of these trends, the denominations have themselves noticed nondenominational strategies. Adjusting for the times, they have adopted a "something for everyone" approach, borrowing elements from other movements and non-movements to attract congregants and remain relevant. Increasingly, there are meditation sessions in Reform communities, mysticism classes in Reconstructionist synagogues, rock bands at Conservative services, movie nights at Chabad houses, and so on. Among communities guided by *halakha* (Jewish law), there is Open Orthodoxy, which emphasizes open-mindedness, expanded roles for women, and a concern for all Jews, and Sephardic initiatives that promote and build upon a history of tolerance and inclusion. Pluralistic and interdenominational organizations, such as the Wexner Foundation and the National Jewish Center for Learning and Leadership (Clal), bring leaders of different stripes together to engage in issues pertinent to *k'lal Yisrael*—all Jews. Non-profits work-

---

[3] Pew Research Center, "A Portrait of Jewish Americans," October 1, 2013, https://www.pewforum.org/wp-content/uploads/sites/7/2013/10/jewish-american-full-report-for-web.pdf

ing across the denominations advocate for marginalized sub-groups, including LGBTQI+, Jews of color, and the disabled. As these efforts attest, Judaism does not exist in a vacuum, but evolves and adapts to the changing world and changing needs of the Jewish people.

On an institutional level, the softening of ideological positions is chronicled in the guiding principles of Reform Judaism. The movement's Pittsburgh Platform of 1885 presented Judaism as a "universal" religion, culture, and ethical system (as opposed to a particularistic "nation"), and rejected dietary restrictions, messianic and Zionistic aspirations, notions of an afterlife, and other "antiquated" trappings of Jewish thought and practice. The Columbus Platform of 1937, composed at a time of growing antisemitism in Europe and American, paints Zionism, ritual observance, and Jewish peoplehood in a more positive light. The Pittsburgh Platform of 1999 broke radically from the denomination's historical roots, affirming comparatively traditionalist positions on God, Torah, and Israel, and signaling a departure from ideological purity.

A loosening of founding ideals goes hand-in-hand with a desire to please as many Jews as possible—particularly as fewer than one-fifth attend services regularly.[4] Such changes are as much top-down decisions as they are bottom-up inevitabilities. As time passes, ascribing to a denomination's core principles becomes less important than finding a suitable community, no matter its affiliation or non-affiliation. Very often, other factors are more pressing than whatever philosophical or ritual concerns a person might have: convenience of location and schedule, connections to clergy or congregants, cost of membership, educational or programmatic offerings, social justice or environmental action projects, perceived status of membership, quality of the *oneg* or *kiddush* (food after services), and so on.

A blurring of denominations can also occur on a microlevel, within small groups, *chavurot* (fellowships), independent congregations, and even individuals. Various portmanteaus have been coined to address this phenomenon: conservadox and orthative (Conservative + Orthodox); conformadox and reservadox (Conservative + Reform + Orthodox); reconservadox (Reconstructionist + Conservative + Orthodox);

---

[4] Ibid.

conservaform and reformative (Conservative + Reform); reformadox (Reform + Orthodox); flexidox (Orthodox but *halakhically* flexible); jagnostic (Jewish + agnostic); jatheist (Jewish + atheist); and others.[5] Moreover, a person might be a member of two or more differently affiliated congregations, bouncing between them for services, programs, and events.

Synagogues sometimes cater to different *minhagim* (customs) under a single roof, usually because of a merger of two congregations, an influx of members from a synagogue that closed, or simply because there is only one *shul* in town. There might be a Reform service on Friday night and a Conservative service on Saturday morning, each with different *siddurim* (prayer books), and congregants might attend one or the other or both. Many synagogues lean toward a denomination, use a denomination's *siddur*, or self-identify with a denominational label, but are not formally affiliated—usually because official membership is financially out of reach. Some try to bring factions together with compromise phrases, such as "Traditional Reform," "Inclusive Orthodox," or "Liberal Conservative." Others are expressly nondenominational, such as Nashuva and IKAR in Los Angeles and the Kitchen in San Francisco.

These trends are part of a broader shift away from the essentialism, absolutism, and grand narratives of post-Enlightenment Modernism, which birthed the Jewish denominations, and into a Postmodern phase, where nuance, curiosity, and self-directedness are, for many, key elements of Jewish identity. This cultural moment is not limited to the Jewish world. Denominational affiliation among American Christians is declining, with both Protestantism and Catholicism experiencing losses. Meanwhile, all categories of the religiously unaffiliated—a group demographers call "nones"—are growing, with those self-describing as "nothing in particular" comprising 17% of the population.[6] Unsurprisingly, decreasing rates of affiliation coincide with declining attendance at worship services. As a result, many

---

[5] See Tim Stewart, *Mixed Blessing: The Dictionary of Blended Words for Religious Identities, Practices, and Beliefs*, https://www.mixedblessingsdictionary.com/blog/

[6] "In U.S., Decline of Christianity Continues at Rapid Pace," Pew Research Center, October 17, 2019, https://www.pewforum.org/2019/10/17/in-u-s-decline-of-christianity-continues-at-rapid-pace/

mainline churches are, like many synagogues, deemphasizing denominational allegiances, reaching out to the "just Christians" and the "spiritual but not religious," and borrowing strategies from across the Christian spectrum and beyond.

The Purpose of this Book

Nondenominational and transdenominational Jewish seminaries fit comfortably in the current climate. These include the Academy for Jewish Religion in Yonkers, New York (est. 1956), the Academy for Jewish Religion California in Los Angeles (est. 2000), rabbinical and cantor-educator programs at Hebrew College in Newton Centre, Massachusetts (est. 2003 and 2004), the new online Pluralistic Rabbinical Assembly, and others. Training across Jewish denominations was once the American norm. The rabbinical schools of Hebrew Union College (est. 1875) and the Jewish Theological Seminary (est. 1886) began with aspirations of producing clergy to serve *k'lal Yisrael*, as did the country's first cantorial program, the School of Sacred Music at Hebrew Union College (est. 1948). This original goal eventually gave way to denominational alignments, which dovetailed with American Judaism's strongly denominational character through the twentieth century. Although denominational schools still hold a prominent place in the American Jewish landscape, they do not have a monopoly. The founders of unaffiliated seminaries have identified a need, found a niche, and are thriving into the twenty-first century.

The chapters that follow present the varied experiences and perspectives of Jewish clergy, scholars, and innovators who study, serve, and teach in pluralistic/inclusive and non/trans/post/interdenominational settings. Some of the authors are themselves grounded in movements or denominations. Others would be hard-pressed to choose an allegiance, or would consider such a choice superfluous in our postmodern milieu. While a few of the essays take a theoretical or historical view of the topic, most are practical in nature, offering ways of making Judaism relevant—both personally and communally—at a time when denominational labels are, for many, inadequate, limiting, or irrelevant. In this sense, the book is more of a "practical guide" than a stuffy philosophical tome.

Part one, "Institutions," recounts the origins, evolutions, and intricacies of the transdenominational Academy for Jewish Religion California and the pluralistic Academy for Jewish Religion in New York. Part two, "Philosophies," provides theoretical and practical frameworks for reaching between and beyond the denominations. Part three, "Journeys," offers personal stories of scholars and practitioners who have traversed the denominations, but do not reside in any of them. Part four, "Teaching," discusses the unique challenges and opportunities of teaching specific subjects—Bible, liturgy, and entrepreneurship—in transdenominational and interdenominational seminary settings. Part five, "Communities," explores applications of pluralism and inclusion in Jewish communal settings.

This book should resonate with readers who are similarly attracted to or engaged in the broad spectrum of ideas and customs that make up the complex and multifarious thing called "Judaism." The chapters are especially useful to Jewish seminary students, graduates, instructors and administrators, synagogue professionals and lay leaders, and students and scholars of American Judaism. Far from the final word on the subject, this book is a modest and timely contribution to a much larger conversation—or perhaps the beginning of a conversation—concerning the present and future of American Jewish life and those who lead it.

Nondenominational Judaism

Part 1

Institutions

Transdenominational Judaism
Stephen Robbins

Almost twenty years ago my fellow traveler and colleague, Rabbi Stan Levy, and I joined forces to innovate a new Jewish institution. Both of us had been asked to teach and ordain lay leaders in the community. *Chutzpadik* (audacious) at its core, we knew something greater needed to be birthed, a seminary unlike anything the West Coast had seen. The denominations had their schools, but for many whose paths had taken them off the conventional roadmap, something new and different was being called into reality. Both Stan and I had followed unconventional paths, created new synagogues, and shared a long history. Stan also saw the Jewish world through what he called "pluralistic" eyes, and I saw it through "transdenominational" eyes—both of which led us to a vision of educating and preparing Jewish clergy to serve in nondenominational communities, as well as many who have found a place in denominational synagogues throughout the country.

And so, after a fortuitous conversation with the dean of the East Coast rabbinic seminary, the Academy for Jewish Religion, the West Coast branch, the Academy for Jewish Religion California, was formed. Though we soon parted ways, the name remains ours, and this maverick enterprise remains stronger than ever. Many were shocked when, in our thirteenth year, we received accreditation from the Western Association of Schools and Colleges and attained a respected place among the other West Coast Jewish seminaries. This recognition, along with our over one hundred fifty graduates, has proven that Stan's and my vision was more than a fantasy or a dream. We created a unique and necessary home, where predominantly second-career students and emerging young leaders with vast experiences and diverse backgrounds could study, thrive, and grow together, ready to confront a changing Jewish world.

My own journey to transdenominational Judaism began when I undertook a job while completing my last years at the Hebrew Union College—a strange development, given that my education trained me to serve Reform Jews. I became the acting Hillel director in Cincinnati, not realizing that my calling would be challenged and my Jewish background severely questioned. The unique character of Hillel, found on college campuses throughout North America, straddles every possible form of Jewish identity: denominational, feminist, anti-war, right wing, secular, cultural, fringe, skeptical, scientific, new-age hippie, and intellectually challenging. Jewish students on the campus not only bring their familial and denominational backgrounds with them, but they also learn, experience, question, and often rebel against convention. Some are looking for familiarity, support, and social connections far from home. Hillel becomes a beacon for like-minded *chavruta* (partnership) and for Jewish leadership to support or challenge existing ways of Jewish expression. For others, typical of young adults, they are questioning and searching to form their own unique identities.

Being a Hillel director made me face the multiplicity and complexity of Jewish possibilities and how to navigate serving them all. The awareness occurred in one single moment that I now realize crystallized the concept and process of a transdenominational approach to Judaism. The transformative moment occurred, as they all do, when I faced my own limitations. It all began the first Shabbat service I was to lead in the fall of 1969. Seeing dozens of students sitting, waiting to meet their new rabbi, I silently picked up the Shabbat prayer book. To my shock, it was the old Silverman prayer book used in Conservative synagogues, with which I had little experience (and only as a congregant). I didn't know the *nusach* (modal prayer chant) of traditionalist communities. Instead, I came prepared, with my guitar, to lead a creative, Shlomo Carlebach-style service. I realized, to my embarrassment and shame, that I didn't know how to lead a service for all Jews, or even how to speak to them in their multiplicity of languages (spiritual or religious). I felt stuck. I had been educated into a box that isolated me from the rest of the Jewish world. I was exclusively a Reform rabbi.

This realization overwhelmed me with sadness and frustration, questioning all my training and experiences over those ten years. The edifice of my identity as a "rabbi" collapsed. I wanted to escape, run from Hillel, and resign; but in that moment of dawning maturity, I stayed to tell the truth. I put down the prayer book, revealing my feelings and expressing my inadequacies. My moment of revelation was greeted with unexpected acceptance. "Rabbi, this is the first I have ever met a rabbi who was willing to share how he felt instead of how all of us should feel." "Rabbi, this is the first time I feel I can sit with other Jews and not feel I don't belong." We spent the rest of the evening, first in large groups, then in small groups, then dyads, sharing about our different backgrounds, attitudes, and personal Jewish experiences. Each of us expanded our own universe, including Jews of different denominations who could have easily been rejected. It was the greatest gift I could have received, redefining for me the purpose of my rabbinate, which ultimately culminated in AJRCA, bringing together seminary students from all walks of Jewish life.

Transdenominational is a big, cumbersome word, yet for me still best describes AJRCA. It is different from post-denominational, which means that denominations are over and will pass out of existence. The movements, especially in America, will continue to grow, evolve, and be major factors in the development of American and world Judaism. As they are now undergoing their own transformation, they are dealing with the same issues that gave birth to this school. I am grateful for the diversity of Jewish expression in the United States because out of that diversity comes truly adaptive creativity.

Judaism was always meant to be a responsive religion. Rabbinic Judaism was modeled to respond to the issues of each generation, so that the next generation would be prepared to deal with the consequences and set a foundation for the next steps into the future. When Judaism and the Jewish people surrender this creative responsiveness toward the world and toward each other, Judaism becomes rigid, arthritic, and brittle. It is my opinion that we are unfortunately already in that state now. In the early years of my rabbinate, subsequent to my Hillel experience, I discovered that true dialogue and cooperation between the movements, the secular Jewish organizations, and unaffiliated (or even the disaffected) Jews, was relatively easy because the hostility that we are seeing today had not set in. In those early years as a Hillel director, I found it rewarding to work with the broadest variety of Jews—from Chabad to alternative-lifestyle Judaism (now called "renewal"), from believers to secularists and Zionists, assimilationists, and just plain alienated Jews. As the years have passed, these denotations have turned into labels, the labels have turned into boxes, and the boxes have become fortresses from which missiles of hostility, rejection, and even denunciation have been thrown. We are in a great stage of Jewish antipathy—one to the other. The Holy One who brought us together at Sinai must be weeping alone at the top of that mountain. How G-d must cry at seeing the way the words of Torah are used to denounce, castigate, and reject other Jews. Who would have thought that the Torah would become a weapon to demonize other Jews?

For me, the word "transdenominational" is not a judgment of other Jews or other movements. In fact, it is the opposite. For me, it represents an inclusiveness for all Jews who can enter the Great House of Torah and be welcomed and legitimated in all of their approaches. In this view I am being neither Pollyanna-like nor messianic. I do not expect the differences between Jewish views to disappear into one single approach to Judaism. This would be a disaster from my perspective, for then Judaism's fundamental creativity and responsiveness to the changing realities of this universe and our lives on this planet would cease. What I hope to abolish is the climate of hostility, separateness, rejection, and isolation that exists among the Jewish people. That can only happen when Jews are able to study together, pray together, and socialize together with not only an openness but a curiosity about the other and how they live. I realize that this will never be a perfect vision come true, but it is fascinating that, without putting a label on it, the majority of American Jews have already become transdenominational.

In my experiences on campus, in synagogues, and within Jewish institutions, as well as my work in alternative Jewish community structures like *chavurot*, independent study groups, independent synagogues, etc., I see the rank and file of the Jewish community not only crossing the boundaries but "shattering" them. Whether it was Carlebach's House of Love and Prayer, Reb Zalman's study groups, the shift in membership from Reform to Conservative synagogues and back again—or the shift from Orthodox to Conservative and back again—the average Jew has voted with his or her feet. The most recent population studies on American Jews, such as Pew's 2013 "Portrait of American Jews," demonstrate that only a small proportion are drawn to synagogues by either ideology, observance, or practice. Increasingly, there is a non-Jewishly educated, secularized, and mobile mass of Jews for whom current Jewish practices and observances may be a barrier to inclusion and involvement. Stan and I were aware of these trends when we founded AJRCA two decades ago. We recognized that training Jewish clergy to reach out to the unaffiliated would be a growing need as the twenty-first century progressed.

It is also true that Jews who are somewhat knowledgeable move back and forth between the movements and ideologies much more easily, with the exception of those who tend to be more doctrinaire and judgmental—both on the far right and the far left of Jewish opinion. As I spent much time speaking to these Jews about their identifications, it became clear to me that they are already nondenominational Jews who are seeking a transdenominational approach that will include the possibility of multiple facets of Jewish experience.

Among the things that seem most attractive to a wide spectrum of Jews—where they can cross boundaries and be inclusive of the non-Jewishly educated—is Torah study. Jewish texts, or text-study from a Jewish approach, is becoming interesting to more and more Jews. It also appears what interests Jews is not so much the study of the text as the mind of the teacher. Those who come to study Torah are increasingly drawn to those who can see both the specific and broad implications and applications of Torah study from a variety of sources and perspectives. So, we return to the beginning again, as always, back to Torah as the heart of Judaism.

Torah opens the hearts and the minds of Jews to the vast array of commentaries and correlative texts. The study of a particular verse or passage unlocks the world of Torah wisdom developed by rabbis and commentators throughout the millennia. That is why a transdenominational view of the study of text is actually more demanding than the denominational process. The study of Torah involves not only knowledge of the text and the various commentaries that accompany it, but also the ideology that guides the teacher. Like my experience with the *siddur* (prayer book) in Hillel, we can be educated into a box in our view of Torah. For me, the mystical/Kabbalistic commentaries (both old and new) guide my understanding in unique and inspiring ways, which—along with form-critical analysis, traditional, modern, psychological, and even a scientific approach—are valid and true. When I study and teach Torah it is from the perspective that all of the "box approaches" are true, that they come from different systems of thinking, and while they may at times be even contradictory, I revel in the increasingly expansive ways in which we can enter into the heart of any text. That experience is never truer than in our study of texts at AJRCA. A seminary whose faculty includes clergy and scholars from every denomination and philosophical bent offers its students a multiplicity of approaches and understandings that, in turn, enrich their toolbox as they go out to teach in the Jewish community.

This inclusiveness of opinions is the hallmark of the development of Jewish thought, as Talmud expresses when it includes both the majority and minority opinions. Oral Law itself was an innovation in a world where Torah stood at the center of the people, and so we continue that tradition by learning the varied systems of thought that comprise the Jewish intellectual, emotional, and mystical experience of interfacing with G-d's Word—the text of Torah and her commentaries.

The basis of a transdenominational view of textual studies begins in a commentary from b. Sanhedrin 34a: "*K'patish yefotzeitz sela shivim panim l'Torah*"—"As a hammer shatters a rock into many sparks so there are 70 faces of Torah." I see this as breaking the text into two parts. The first implies that the Torah has an outer covering which must be shattered. The second is the sparks of light, which are released into the world from the core of the G-d-Presence contained within. This reveals the 70 faces, or *panim*. I suggest that the word *panim* can also be understood as *eyes*, *doors*, or *facets*. *Eyes* because the sparks enable one to see into the inner core of Torah, while at the same time one can see the truths in the world around us, which are illuminated by the sparks of Torah. *Doors* in that striking the rock creates an opening through which one can enter the core of

Torah and bear her truth outward into the world. And *facets* in that Torah is like a great diamond constantly being cut and polished with an infinite number of angles. Like the diamond cutters, "spiritual" diamond cutters come to the great rock of Torah, and through study and explicating the text, strike sparks from her very core. The sparks enter each facet and turn it into a vessel of knowledge and light. Each student brings a unique ideology, experience, and approach to Torah that creates another doorway through which the light of Torah can be revealed outward. The light shines in its own unique vector into a part of the world which is dark until the door, or facet, is opened. All these different approaches to text are themselves part of a greater truth. Together, they eventually make a whole truth that, please G-d, shall come to us before it is too late.

The transdenominational approach to text should be that which unites us with a common purpose, but with a diversity of thought and action that makes it possible to reveal more and more doors into the great diamond of the Torah, so that her light may shine on us. Transdenominational Judaism represents an inclusiveness for all Jews who can enter the Great House of Torah and be welcomed and legitimate in all its approaches. It is why I believe this pathway is shaped by the particularly important midrash, cited above, about the 70 faces of Torah. This is the fundamental image at the foundation of the transdenominational approach to Jewish study and Jewish life. The process of shattering the rock to reveal the 70 faces of Torah has been the greatest metaphor for "shattering" the conventional training of rabbis, cantors, and chaplains.

Our purpose is to unify, based on two rabbinic sayings: "All Jews have a stake in the world to come" ("*Kol Yisrael, yesh lahem chelek l'olam ha-bah*") and "Every Jew is responsible one for the other" ("*Kol Yisrael arevim zeh la-zeh*"). Both sayings teach us that every Jew has a portion both in this world and the next, with a legitimate right and responsibility to carve Torah for themselves. Torah was given to all of us at Mount Sinai—to those who were there in that moment, as well as all Jews past and future. All of us have an equal stake in Torah. Every Jew is responsible for the other in bringing the words of Torah from underneath her mantle and into the world. This also means that we are responsible, one for the other, in making sure that Torah can be studied and made accessible to every Jew. We must not exclude Jews from the study of Torah regardless of their personal practice, knowledge, temperament, or ideological bent. In fact, we must interact with those who are different from us, for that is where Torah lives and breathes.

The training of rabbis, cantors, chaplains, and other Jewish professionals is informed by the reality of assimilation and denomination. Institutional Judaism has lost roughly 70 percent of Jews in America. Their lack of participation does not mean that they are not Jewish; it just means that they are not interested in the ways in which Judaism has been presented. I suggest that the 70 facets of Torah are the best medicine for the alienated 70 percent of Jews.

This reality is ever so real today as it was twenty years ago, when I first articulated my philosophy of transdenominational Judaism. The initial concept has proven to be an exciting premise—even for the denominations. We have found that clergy and professional leaders in the denominations are applying transdenominational teachings and practices within their work settings. I was recently invited to a seminar at American Jewish University, a Conservative institution, on various denominational approaches to education. I was quite surprised to learn that I was not going to be participating in the morning panel, which included rabbis of all the denominations, but leading a workshop, alone, on transdenominational Judaism. It seemed that AJRCA represented the quintessential model for the future of educating all Jews, including lay people and clergy. The participants shared with me that they, too, had been on a journey of interdenominational study and transformation. I feel very grateful that our work at AJRCA has been inspirational not only to those who study with us, but also in the Jewish community at large.

In these intervening twenty years, there have been other organizations whose approaches reflect a multi-denominational or transdenominational philosophy. Among those are other seminaries, such as Boston Hebrew College, and of course AJR in New York (which predates our existence by decades), Clal (National Jewish Center for Learning and Leadership), and the Institute for Jewish Spirituality.

This is a growing movement that began with Reb Zalman and Reb Shlomo, and has led many of us on a journey of expanding our vision of contemporary Jewish life.

Below are the principles of transdenominational Judaism as I see them, and how they have laid the foundation for AJRCA and its growth.

1. All the denominations and movements within contemporary Jewry are valid and provide purposeful Jewish education and spiritual experience.

2. There is no competition between the denominations as to which is right and which is wrong. Each offers a unique pathway of learning and lifestyle for a segment of contemporary Jewry who are drawn to that approach and are comfortable in it.

3. We do not live in a post-denominational era, but must strive for an integrated tapestry of the teachings and experiences provided by each denomination.

4. The prefix "trans" in transdenominational refers to a yet unformed, greater expression of contemporary Jewry and Judaism that will grow out of this inclusionary approach.

5. Clergy and professional leaders who follow this path are committed to serving Jews wherever they find them, rather than serving institutions or ideologies.

6. Transdenominational Judaism is committed to the spiritual, psychological, and behavioral growth of each Jew as a pathway to fulfillment and meaningful living.

7. This path of education for Jewish clergy and professionals is still developing a coherent pedagogy. It behooves AJRCA—and perhaps other such seminaries—to inquire into the experience of teaching in this unique academic setting, so that courses truly reflect the multi-denominational character and sources for education and inspiration of its graduates and ordinees.

8. This path is not meant to be a movement, but rather a template for ongoing development and transformation of American Jewry.

9.   The goal of the training rabbis, cantors, chaplains, and other leaders should be, in part, to reach out to those Jews to whom the conventional denominations do not speak.

10. The faculty of the Academy is committed to interdenominational discussion and study in order to continually refine and articulate this philosophy in practical application, so that the graduates and ordinees can maximize their own personal skills and talents in the Jewish world.

Graduates who leave AJRCA will, I believe, make Torah and living Judaism accessible to many Jews. For some it will be in their synagogue settings, and for others it will be in their enterprising approach to bringing Judaism to the people in new communities, new institutions, new music and artwork, through the internet, or through the written word. With so many Jews who are unaffiliated, new, creative, and innovative approaches to teaching and preaching are necessary to fulfill the need of those who decline to be part of a religious institution. AJRCA, with its transdenominational foundation, is preparing Jewish leaders of the future to teach, reach, and inspire Jews (and non-Jews) throughout the world.

Transdenominational Origins
Mel Gottlieb

In the year 2000, Rabbi Stan Levy called me and asked if I would be interested in joining the Academy for Jewish Religion California (AJRCA), a new rabbinic school that would be operating with a novel approach heretofore untested. It would be an attempt to educate students in all denominations, culling from the best ideas and practices of each of the denominations, and to reach out to those who are non-affiliated. The school would also contain a spiritual component that would guide the psycho-spiritual character of the student in addition to the scholarly dimension of textual mastery. Moreover, the school would attract many second-career students by scheduling classes on a three-day-per-week basis.

The idea was intriguing, but I was a bit skeptical about how this might work. How would students from different backgrounds be integrated into an educational program encompassing different philosophies, or create a prayer experience that would be satisfactory to all? Would the classes emphasize a certain denomination at the expense of others due to the proclivity of the instructor? How would a *minyan* (quorum) be constructed with the different styles of prayer in the different denominations? Would there be comfort or dissatisfaction among the student body?

Rabbi Levy explained to me that students had approached him to help form a new kind of rabbinic program, one that included a deep spiritual emphasis in addition to the academic emphasis that they had found in other schools. The students who would enroll would be a self-selected group looking for such a program; a mature group who would be more open to this experimentation and likely more flexible to participate in this idealistic endeavor. Their passion would overcome their practical sense, for students who were looking for a secure traditional school would not even consider this new experiment. It would only be an individual who had a strong passion for a spiritual experience as well as a scholarly experience who would take a risk on such a program. This school would not be for the practical minded;

for jobs could not be assured, there was no accreditation to be found, and it might be challenging to attract a highly respected faculty.

So I told him that, while I was deeply appreciative of his thinking of me, I would need some time to think this over. I did not join the faculty until the second semester of AJRCA's existence. It was only after I was approached several more times that this endeavor gripped my soul. I then asked for a list of which faculty members had joined and the makeup of the curriculum. It was explained to me that the curriculum was being created by examining the curricula of all the current rabbinic programs, including the essential courses from those schools, and adding some new creative, spiritual classes in Hasidut, Kabbalah, and Mussar. There would be eight categories of study and the students would have to take a minimum number of courses in each of the categories: Bible, rabbinics, Jewish history, Jewish thought, Jewish liturgy, professional skills, Hebrew, and Jewish mysticism and spiritual traditions.

As for the faculty, the selection of scholars had to be of the highest caliber in order to attract students to such a startup program. Several prominent individuals had expressed interest. After careful consideration and deliberation, I decided to join this creative and, indeed, necessary new educational "experiment." Deep down, I thought it would be a miracle for AJRCA to succeed as a newcomer on the block competing with other prestigious, established schools—but miracles do happen.

On a spiritual and philosophical level, I was personally disturbed by the current trend in our Jewish community which emphasized the importance of a denomination at the expense of the unity of the Jewish community. There was an understanding and a commitment to show loyalty to the expectations of each denomination, and inevitably an erection of strong boundaries in each system that inhibited change and dialogue with other denominations; thus I imagined future entropy in these denominational entities. I wondered how it might be possible for each disparate group to share the uniqueness of its traditions with each other and thus grow in wisdom and potential fellowship. I imagined that if young people could see our cooperation and respect for each other while maintaining the unique insights found in our separate traditions, they would indeed perceive us more as a "spiritual people," an *Am Kadosh*, rather than a series of elitist groups more committed to their own existence and success than the growth and survival of our larger Jewish community. Studies were emerging showing the decline in membership in our synagogues, and that our young people were drifting away from Jewish education and seeking meaning and spiritual fulfillment in other traditions. Thus, I concluded that this new "experiment" would be a worthy project to join and build, as it might bring a new, necessary, vital voice to our Jewish community.

In the early history of our school, we began in partnership with the Academy for Jewish Religion in New York, since that school was based on a pluralistic model. However, after two years, we separated our affiliation with the New York school because our curriculum included courses that did not fit its educational model. We required courses in Hasidut, Kabbalah, and Mussar—which were beyond the norm of their offerings, and too "West Coasty" for the particular taste of the New York school. We decided to part ways in order to retain our autonomy and freedom in creating a unique curriculum that would fit the model we were trying to form—a model that included an exploration of the mystical and spiritual traditions found in our literature and history. We were committed to allowing our students to explore their inner rhythms and beliefs, and grow in relation to texts that explore these possibilities.

In the early years, Rabbi Jack Schechter did a wonderful job as dean of the rabbinic school, gathering in new faculty members and putting together the early curriculum. I became dean of students at the time, and worked together with our three co-founders, Rabbi Stan Levy, Rabbi Steve Robbins, and Rabbi Mordecai Finley, to further develop the curriculum. Over a two-year period, we met bi-weekly and developed a sequence of courses in each of the eight categories of study. We were happily surprised at the caliber of students who had entered the school, and our reputation began to grow as a school that had a very warm, affirming faculty, and a student body that respected and encouraged each other. The outer community was surprised that many recognized scholars had joined our faculty and that advanced students from different parts of the country were attending. In our early days, it was hard to receive approbation from the denominational schools, as there was a natural response to a "newcomer" that was entering a pasture that had a limited number of applicants. The new nondenominational model was also threatening, as it had the potential to attenuate the strong affiliations of the denominational movements. Though we expressed that our philosophy was not to diminish the existing movements, but to add another possibility for those outside of the denominational reality, the anxiety persisted that we may be taking potential students away from their schools. It was our conviction that different students would have different preferences, and that there would be room for growth in all the schools. But, in the early years, there was an attempt to block our graduates from entering the Los Angeles Board of Rabbis and an instruction to movement synagogues to only hire graduates from their own seminaries.

After Rabbi Jack Schechter completed his tenure as dean of the rabbinic school, I took over that post in 2004. Our school was growing, new faculty members were hired, and students were attracted to our three-day-a-week program that enabled them to continue to work part-time.

In the next few years I instituted a Mussar program as part of our curriculum to train professional clergy to develop heightened self-awareness and increase their effectiveness as leaders. I believe it was the first accelerated growth program of its kind to promote a heightened consciousness in future Jewish clergy. The new program was intended to enhance character development using the texts and practices of the Mussar movement that R. Yisrael Salanter introduced in the nineteenth century. On Sunday evenings for three years, groups of six to eight students would study Mussar for one hour. The group leaders were selected from students who had demonstrated leadership capacity, taken a course on Mussar, and received some training with me. After each Mussar group session, I met with the group leaders in a supervisory session for an hour to review their group meeting. In these sessions, we reviewed the process and dynamics within the groups, and the challenges and progress of each of the students. As noted, every two weeks the students would concentrate on a character trait taken from a Mussar text, study the trait, and read about it in Mussar texts—but more importantly become aware of how that trait affected them. They were asked to reflect on this *middah* (trait) and enter their perceptions in a journal. When they came together to meet on Sunday evenings, each student would share their experiences and insights, and support the experiences of each of the other students in the group. Their reading material included an article I had written for the journal *Tradition* some years ago summarizing the highlights and goals of the movement, as well as *Everyday Holiness* by Alan Morinis, and Moshe Chaim Luzatto's *Path of the Just*. This became a vital part of our curriculum and contributed to the psycho-spiritual development of students in our school.

In addition to our rabbinic school, we also opened the only cantorial school on the West Coast under the deanship of Cantors Nate Lam and Perryne Anker. Many prominent cantors in the Los Angeles community joined the faculty and the school flourished. Our cantorial alumni currently hold positions in major synagogues in Los Angeles, the surrounding areas, and beyond.

In the early 2000s, *The Jewish Journal of Greater Los Angeles* published an article about the shortage of Jewish chaplains in Los Angeles, predicting that the situation would only get worse due to the increase of the elderly population in the coming years. Jewish chaplains at that time were comprised mainly of retired rabbis and lay-volunteers. The article implied that the clients were not being served in the professional manner they deserved, and that training of the lay-chaplains was insufficient to serve the Jewish community.

As a result, I introduced the idea of AJRCA creating a professional chaplaincy program and developed a curriculum for such a school. I was appointed dean of the chaplaincy school at the time, based on my background in social work, psychology, and years of counseling others. Once more, the Board of Rabbis had reservations about our launching this program, as they were in charge of finding job placements for retired rabbis who were eager to continue their service to others. It was also economically advantageous to hospitals such as Cedars Sinai to continue to train lay-chaplains rather than hire professionally trained chaplains. But we decided that it was essential to offer professional training for the sake of the clients. In 2007, we began a clinical pastoral education (CPE) program in the chaplaincy school under the guidance of Rabbi Rochelle Robins. This allowed our graduates to receive certification as Jewish chaplains by completing the necessary units in CPE.

Rabbi Robins eventually became the dean of the school in 2012. Under her leadership, our chaplaincy school has grown in prominence; our chaplains report much soul satisfaction in their work, while also fulfilling an essential need in Los Angeles and elsewhere. I believe our school has contributed to the elevation of the importance and stature of the chaplaincy profession.

An important turning point for our school occurred in 2013, when we received accreditation from the Western Association of Schools and Colleges (WASC). This was quite an accomplishment to achieve in such a short period of time. The WASC visiting team complimented our school for its academic excellence, its creativity, student and faculty satisfaction, and its contribution to the Jewish community. They also acknowledged our new Master of Jewish Studies Program developed by Dr. Tamar Frankiel and Cantor Jonathan Friedmann.

As our school grew through the years, we encountered several challenges. As we anticipated, our morning *minyan* presented a challenge because of the different backgrounds and levels of experience of incoming students. Some were more comfortable with Orthodox and Conservative services and some with Reform and Renewal services. Their memories and attachments to specific services aroused *kavanah* (intentionality) in participation in their familiar services, but discomfort in participation in newly encountered services. There was also some conflict about whether the services should be run as teaching and learning experiences, or actual prayer services without interruptions. At times, we experimented with having a combination of models: some learning services and some straight prayer services. Different student prayer-leaders would lead the weekly service in the model they were accustomed to, such that one week there might be an Orthodox service and the following week a Reform service, etc. Neither solution fulfilled the need of many students. Currently, we have a model where the first six weeks we have teaching and learning minyanim, and the rest of the year students lead different models of services, so that students are exposed to different styles and customs. It works relatively well, but still remains challenging.

Another issue emerged due to the three-day-a-week schedule in which a number of classes are offered at similar times during the day, e.g., three classes offered at 9:00 A.M. Students are forced to choose one course and may have to wait until the following year—or the year after that—to take the other courses in the same time slot. Moreover, the abundance of courses in a short period of time precludes sufficient breaks between classes for relaxation and interactions between students, which can also increase learning. We are currently considering expanding our course offerings to additional days to address the problem.

A final challenge is the cost of room and board for out-of-towners who fly in to attend classes. This affects our enrollment, and causes great stress in our students.

We have begun to address the scheduling and travel dilemmas by introducing a model of online courses as part of our school offerings. By enabling students to attend classes synchronously online, rather than travel a long distance to school, we have alleviated the burden of travel and expense, and also expanded options in scheduling for students. We were apprehensive of the negative impact this new model might have on the warmth and interaction of our student body. However, we were happily surprised to discover that this model could work with a creative addition of a "hybrid" model, which requires all online students to attend three-day on-site educational experiences as part of their program. The first residency period occurs in the opening week of the fall semester. The bonding that occurs between students enables them to continue to build their relationships through the year. They meet again for three days during the middle of the year and three days on the last week of the spring semester. By the end of the year, most students develop meaningful relationships with one other.

Each class contains both distance and on-site students, and the instructor is able to pay attention to both groups at the same time. Those on-screen and those in the room share with each other, engage in dialogue, and experience a rich educational experience. When they meet in person for the three sessions throughout the year, there is great joy and eagerness to interact with one another, and they have accepted this modality as an alternative that works for them better than they (and we) imagined. This new addition to our program makes it possible for students from many parts of the state, country, and world to study with us.

As these past two decades have unfolded, we feel optimistic that our transdenominational enterprise is reaching its initial goals. We were concerned about the disparity and bifurcation of our Jewish community, and now we feel a greater unity through this model. We see that many denominational schools are entertaining a more pluralistic language in their marketing and course offerings, and are reaching out to their fellow Jews and communities with a clarion call for more unity. We believe that our initial vision is essential to building stronger ties in our community, and that this model is very appealing to non-affiliated Jews and young people who are looking for a spiritual dimension in their religious studies. We are deeply satisfied that we held to our conviction that introducing new courses in our curriculum—such as Hasidut, Kabbalah, and Mussar—were beneficial to the atmosphere in the school and the spiritual maturity and wisdom of our graduates.

Our students and more than 150 alumni have achieved many leadership positions in synagogues, day schools, boards of rabbis, hospitals, nursing homes, hospices, and more throughout the Los Angeles area and beyond. This is evidence that our new transdenominational model is not only effective, but also sought after by many Jewish institutions in our country. We hope this path will continue to grow in the future.

Living Pluralism
Ora Horn Prouser

Four years ago, in celebration of its 60th anniversary, the Academy for Jewish Religion in Yonkers, New York, published a book on Jewish pluralism.[1] For that volume, I wrote a chapter laying out AJR's approach to pluralism and how it affects our community, our students, our religious life, and our curriculum. I reprint that article below with a new postscript, as it is a fitting contribution to this volume's celebration of nondenominational Jewish community and education.

Publishing a book on pluralism has been a goal at the Academy for Jewish Religion (AJR), located in Yonkers, New York, for many years. It is thus with particular pleasure and pride that we see the realization of this dream. The term "pluralism" has become a buzzword in contemporary Jewish culture with a variety of denominational, post-denominational, and other communities describing themselves as pluralistic. Each of these communities has a different definition of pluralism, and each tries to emphasize their pluralism as a positive attribute of the organization.

It is understandable why each of these communities tries to identify as pluralistic, as much of the larger Jewish world now sees pluralism as a key approach to Jewish life in particular, and to the larger world in general. At AJR we have a very distinct approach to pluralism that goes beyond what most of these communities describe. After all, AJR has been a living laboratory of pluralism for the past sixty years. At AJR, students study together, pray together, and function as a community despite (or perhaps because of) their great variety of backgrounds, approaches, and understandings of Jewish life. It is therefore instructive to share AJR's understanding of pluralism and what it means.

The question has been asked how pluralism compares to diversity, non-denominationalism, post-denominationalism, etc. This is a very

---

[1] Leonard Levin, ed., *Studies in Judaism and Pluralism: Honoring the 60th Anniversary of the Academy for Jewish Religion* (Teaneck, NJ: Ben Yehuda Press, 2016). Thank you to Dr. Leonard Levin and AJR for permission to reprint my essay here.

difficult question, and one that we have thought about quite a bit at AJR. Non-denominationalism and post-denominationalism assume that denominations are no longer relevant or viable. That is not the view at AJR. We have students and alumni in our community who are very much part of denominations. Some in our community feel that they belong in denominations. They choose to be a part of AJR because they recognize that the Jewish world is larger than any one denomination and they want to be comfortably engaged with all facets of the Jewish community, and to truly understand and appreciate all areas. They themselves, however, identify within a specific movement. Thus, AJR's pluralism is not nondenominational or post-denominational.

AJR's approach to pluralism is an appreciation of diversity; but it is much more than that. There are communities claiming to be pluralistic that talk about respect for the other and tolerance of other viewpoints. Again, this does not adequately define the AJR approach to pluralism. Tolerance is necessary, but it is a very low bar for a pluralistic community. Respect is very important, but it, too, is not enough for true pluralism to flourish. AJR's approach to pluralism expects members of our community to cherish one another. Cherishing means that ideas other than your own are valuable and that one can learn from them. Cherishing means that you not only respect others, but you know that your perspective, your life, and your approach to Jewish life are richer and deeper because of your interaction with other views and approaches. A community that cherishes the other knows that each of us benefits from being a part of a pluralistic community—not only in learning about others but in becoming who we want and need to be.

This all sounds positive and growing and enriching; so why wouldn't all communities choose to be pluralistic? The answer is that true pluralism is very difficult. The pluralistic community needs to be aware of many issues, and to be extremely sensitive to individuals and their needs and struggles in a way that is different from communities that are more homogeneous. This leads to another lesson we have learned at AJR about living pluralism. In a community of individuals with many different approaches, there is a tendency for individuals to feel either alone in their views, or concerned that their approach is being ignored. One refrain often heard when meeting with students is that "everyone in the community is (fill in the blank) but me." That is, everyone knows more Hebrew, everyone is more comfortable with prayer, everyone understands what it means to meditate, everyone has studied Talmud, etc. Because students come from so many different backgrounds there is often an unwarranted sense of inadequacy or concern that comes from the worry that other backgrounds and approaches have better prepared students for their studies. While it is true that some students are more prepared for high-level Jewish study than others, our experience is that students bring to the table different strengths and weaknesses and that, in general, students from one or another approach are not generally more suited for rabbinic or cantorial education. The feeling of concern in the face of great diversity is real and needs to be respected and confronted directly. Therefore, there is a need to engage in serious and honest communication, and a need to be willing to speak about ideas and concerns that are minor as well as those that are hot-button issues. Serious communication lodged in a warm and nurturing communal atmosphere allows us at AJR to negotiate a strong communal feeling together with a cherishing of differences. The importance of our community being so loving and warm cannot be emphasized enough. That nurturing and sensitive communal atmosphere provides the perfect backdrop for complicated conversations.

Related to this is another area of concern among members of a pluralistic community. There are misgivings among many that their viewpoint is not being adequately represented and expressed. As an example, during one semester I received the following expressions of concern from students and alumni.

"There are not sufficient members of the faculty who are Reform."

"Orthodox viewpoints are ignored and belittled in communal conversations."

"AJR's policy on not accepting students of patrilineal descent is not befitting a pluralistic institution."

"There is a lack of understanding among the community about the idea of feeling bound by *halakha* (Jewish law)."

What is evident in this brief list is that students and alumni were concerned that their viewpoints were not adequately expressed or represented. Some felt the need to push for their approaches. However, they often did not see that others on very different points on the spectrum, those the complainants presumed to hold dominant or majority views, were feeling the exact same thing. They did not see the parts of our policies that supported their views; they only saw the sides they thought were not representing their own perspectives. Again, the key is strong communication within communal connection.

Living in a pluralistic community means being aware of these difficulties and addressing them. It is easy to say that individuals should not feel that way, but, that is just not understanding human nature. The reality is that pluralistic communities need to be willing to address issues like these head-on, continuously, in order to help individuals see the larger picture. And there are times when it is necessary to step in and be the voice of the truly unvoiced. We have found that as students continue in the program they feel less defensive, more comfortable, and recognize the tremendous benefits of this structure. Being aware of the process of growth, however, is necessary.

It also means listening, as members of the community can make real contributions to addressing these issues. A good example is the observance of *kashrut* (dietary laws) at AJR. The AJR policy on *kashrut* used to be that all public events, and all food meant to be shared, needed to be certified kosher. Food that individuals brought for themselves, however, did not need to be certified kosher. It could not include shellfish, it could not mix milk and meat, and all meat needed to be kosher. This worked as a whole, but students felt frustrated that they could not bring in food to share with their friends and classmates. A student, therefore, suggested a new policy, which has been instituted at AJR. Food at all public events still needs to be certified kosher. However, students are welcome to bring in food to share in the student lounge. Food that is brought in still needs to follow the basic rules of *kashrut*. The food, however, does not need to be certified kosher. The person bringing in the food fills out a form that explains where the food came from. Is it store bought or homemade? If store bought, what kind of store? If homemade, what is the *kashrut* practice where it was made? Are meat and milk dishes kept separate? Is non-kosher food brought into the home? Are dishes washed together? Questions like these are answered and the form is left next to the food. It is then up to each member of the community to decide whether to partake of the items.

While this may seem like a lot of work to put out a plate of brownies, there is something much deeper going on here. This policy shows deep respect for members of the community, making it clear that communal eating can be a part of communal life, even while members of the community have different ways of observing *kashrut*. It makes it clear that the answer is not always to follow the most stringent level of observance, but that there are ways to allow for a variety of approaches to feel accepted. Furthermore, it challenges students to consider how their own personal decisions about religious observance affect fellow Jews. It also leads to important and valuable conversation. Once forms are filled out, members of the community can ask each other, why do they observe the way they do? How does it work for them? These conversations are a beautiful and necessary part of a pluralistic community. These conversations make it clear that individuals with different patterns of practice come to those decisions with deep thought, sincere appreciation for Jewish life, and honest desire to live a godly life. That understanding is not easy to come by in heterogeneous communities, and is of immense value in understanding the larger Jewish world and in cherishing others.

While some may find this uncomfortable, we have found that true pluralism means that everyone is somewhat uncomfortable! An individual may be comfortable with our policy on Jewish identity but uncomfortable with our *kashrut* policy. A second person may be perfectly comfortable with our policy on *kashrut* but uncomfortable with our public prayer. The goal is not to make every person comfortable with each decision. Rather, the goal is to make the discomfort a generative discomfort—one that leads us to think, struggle, push ourselves, and ask important questions.

While we work to make our community extremely inclusive and accepting, we also recognize that pluralism cannot exist without borders. Every pluralistic community needs to also have core values which create borders to that pluralism. AJR, for example, has core values stating that we are egalitarian and LGBTQI+-friendly. If someone believes that for religious reasons he should not hear a woman's voice in song, then he will not feel comfortable being a part of the AJR community, as women's voices are raised in song every day. If someone does not believe that rabbis and cantors should be openly gay, then they may not feel comfortable at AJR. We accept that, and don't claim otherwise. And if someone does not believe that rabbinical students need to engage in years of serious study of Talmud and Codes, then they may not feel comfortable at AJR.

A good example of the need for borders on pluralism was made very clear in a program we ran on patrilineal descent in pluralistic communities. We had some students who expressed that communities should be open and welcoming to everyone, and that Jews of patrilineal descent should be accepted as part of any community. They felt that there was no reason that a community should not accept patrilineal Jews. Some who felt they could not accept patrilineal descent because of their understanding of Jewish law were concerned that their viewpoint was presented as cold and dismissive of important members of our community. In other words, people on both sides felt concern, rejection, and lack of understanding of the other side. It was our job as a community to make clear that while we appreciate all members of our community and cherish all ideas, each community, including each pluralistic community, still needs to make a decision for itself whether they accept patrilineal descent in their community—as they must with a variety of defining issues of practice, identity, and belief. That is setting the borders of the pluralism for that community. There is no way to have a pluralistic community without making those decisions. It is a fallacy to say that a community accepts all ideas for that community. These decisions need to be made. They can be reviewed and amended, but the difficult issues must be addressed.

One of the issues that we have seen in the current state of affairs in pluralism arose during this discussion. A member of our faculty said that she could not imagine any non-Orthodox Jew being upset if their son or daughter married a Jew of patrilineal descent. It was explained to her that for some Jews who consider Jewish law binding, a Jew of patrilineal descent is not considered Jewish. That was not part of her world view, though she considered herself pluralistic. In too many communities, *pluralism* has come to be synonymous with *left wing*. Communities call themselves pluralistic and accepting, but some really do not include more traditional Jewish approaches in that mix. At AJR this is an issue we think about often. While there are certain areas that are liberal in the borders we have chosen for ourselves, beyond those, we absolutely see our community as open to those from all parts of the Jewish world. We always try to have a true variety of opinions presented in our programs and in our courses; yet we acknowledge that the majority of our community is liberal in thought and practice. An interesting case was made to us, however, by a traditional Conservative Jew. He told us that he was actually more comfortable at AJR at this point than at Conservative institutions that have become exceedingly liberal. The point he made was that given that we are pluralistic, there is room for many different viewpoints. He was less comfortable, however, with Conservative institutions that were not making room for traditional approaches. Thus, at least to some people, our pluralistic community is more open to traditional Jews than are denominational environments.

A difficult and essential area of decision making for every pluralistic community is how to engage in communal prayer. Some communities express their pluralism by having multiple *minyanim* (quorums) whenever they engage in prayer, thus making room for many different types of prayer services to occur simultaneously. Often communities separate for all or part of prayer services and then join together for part of the service or for learning or socializing afterwards.

AJR has an approach to *tefillah* (prayer) that is not common else-where—yet. When we pray together we make a covenant as a community to all follow whatever is decided by the prayer leader. The prayer leader decides which prayer book will be used (an assortment is available at all times), and decides what kind of prayer experience we will have. This can be traditional, meditative, musical, primarily movement, or anything else. The liturgy can be more or less tradition-al—including or excluding matriarchs in the *Amidah*, using language of the classical liturgy, the Reform *siddur*, the Reconstructionist *siddur*, etc. The only non-negotiable rules for our services are that each service needs to include a mourner's *Kaddish*, and that parts of the service that traditionally require a *minyan* cannot be included unless a *minyan* is present. This is not to say that everyone enjoys every service equally. There are prayer services that some consider as *halakhically* (legally) fulfilling their requirement to pray, and others they do not consider as *halakhically* fulfilling their requirement to pray. There are some prayer services that various members of the community find uncomfortable, or out of their comfort zone. Yet we *daven* (pray) as a community. We share our experience as a community. We learn from each other. We find elements that are meaningful and fulfilling which, if we only prayed with those like us, we would never have experienced. As a community, we find this approach to be fitting, conducive to spiritual growth, and advantageous to all involved. Speaking personally, I find it to be one of the most beautiful parts of our pluralistic institution.

While this all works well, when a situation arose that an Orthodox faculty member needed to say *Kaddish* for observance of a *yahrzeit* (anniversary of a death), he asked if he could lead and if we would have separate but equal seating for that minyan. The community readily agreed, and there, too, we felt the warmth and comfort of a unified community.

AJR is not only a community who "live" together, dealing with prayer, food, and communal life. We are primarily a community that studies together. Pluralism makes its way into our courses as well. For example, in our liturgy classes, it is important that students learn the traditional liturgy, and then understand how each movement has worked with that liturgy, responded to it, and modified it to suit their theological approaches. In our professional skills classes, students need to learn how to perform ritual ceremonies for all parts of the Jewish community. They need to understand traditional life cycle events, and at the same time, how they are observed by various parts of the Jewish community. They also need to work to determine their own personal practice and ritual parameters and standards in performing life cycle events.

Studying Bible in a pluralistic setting brings its own challenges. In the introductory class we spend time discussing our understandings of revelation. Students may have a variety of approaches to revelation ranging from believing that God wrote the Torah to an understanding that the Torah is the product of purely human hands, and everything in between. Students are given license to maintain their own beliefs in this area, but at the same time, they need to understand the variety of approaches and the implications of and reasons behind them.

As in all areas, studying Bible at AJR would include attention to the Bible as a pluralistic document. While that is not the focus of this paper, it would emphasize that traditional Bible study through the *Miqraot Gedolot* assumes that we study many and conflicting approaches at once. It would include that the biblical text itself includes conflicting approaches, and the like. Our approach to *peshat* (contextual interpretation) and *derash* (interpretive reading as well as ethical, homiletical, mystical approaches, etc.) also supports AJR's pluralistic approach. We emphasize that not only can we have multiple *derash* meanings to the text, we can also have multiple *peshat* readings of the text. In class we emphasize that we can agree or disagree about our reading of text, but that there is not only one legitimate reading. The fact that someone else has a different approach does not negate one's own reading. This approach to reading parallels the approach to AJR's pluralistic living. We can agree or disagree, knowing that we can learn from each other, but that a difference of opinion does not negate either view or either person. It is the text itself that unites us, as well as our shared commitment to that text and the community of learners. It is the text itself, together with our ability to interact with it and within a diverse community, which is one true test of our individual "readings."

AJR has been a living laboratory of pluralism for 60 years. As with all experiments, the validity of the findings is determined by the ability of others to replicate the results. The exponential growth of pluralistic communities, and of interest in the principles of pluralism among organizations and institutions heretofore more narrowly defined, indicates that AJR's 60-year experiment has been a resounding success. It is now our privilege and our mission to offer our experience to an increasingly diverse Jewish community which can grow immeasurably by building upon our findings over the next

60 years. That is a mission of biblical proportions: "120 years…vision undiminished, vigor unabated" (Deut. 34:7).

Postscript

Now that four years have passed, it is only fitting that I have some thoughts to add to this description of AJR's pluralistic identity. One area that we have continued to evolve around is the definition of pluralism. To many, pluralism refers to the Jewish life of the community. In other words, a pluralistic community would bring together individuals from a large number of denominations, and those who feel that they don't fit into any denomination. While that is still very much an important part of our pluralism, we have been speaking a lot lately about a broader definition of pluralism. AJR's pluralism can be felt in many more areas than just religious approach. Our pluralism encompasses gender, sexuality, race, class, age, ability, socioeconomic background, learning style, and much more. Our students range in age from their twenties through their seventies or eighties. Our students are gendered and gender-fluid. We cherish this diversity in the same way we cherish religious pluralism. We are each fuller and stronger religious leaders thanks to this diversity. We cherish the passion of youth and the wisdom that comes with age. We learn from the struggles of individuals who have faced adversity and grow in compassion and understanding. Our religious leaders have fuller understandings of the world and greater empathy for those they will serve thanks to our rich and deep community of learners. This, too, is pluralism.

From a curricular standpoint, our pluralism comes through in our understanding of what can be involved in rabbinic and cantorial education. What has been true from the outset was that by attending a pluralistic seminary, each student willingly commits to exposing themselves and delving into areas they may feel are not going to be part of their clergy work. For example, students who come to us from a more liberal background and who claim they will not need to be well versed in Talmud for their practical work are nonetheless required to take the full three years of Talmud courses. Students who come to us from a more traditional background and who feel that there will not be room in their community for contemporary spiritual experimentation and creation of innovative ritual are nonetheless required to take the Architecture of Ritual course in addition to other courses in our Spirituality curriculum. Although some may feel that these courses are outside of their purviews, what we know from our history and from our alumni is that a pluralistic education prepares clergy for the fullest connection to Jewish communities, and that everyone—the rabbi, the cantor, and the community members—benefits from this broadening perspective.

We have further expanded this work in our new curricular work. Our pluralistic philosophy allows us to think very broadly about what unusual areas will better prepare our rabbis and cantors to serve the contemporary Jewish community. For example, our new cantorial program includes an emphasis on Peace Studies. Using sacred Jewish texts, the progression of these courses takes students from an introductory examination of war and peace, conflict and agreement, to the experience of building communities both locally and on the world stage, and finally to using the human voice in the service of conflict resolution. This is not simply an elective track. These courses are required of all cantorial students.

In another area, we have been using the arts as a vehicle for delving into text study in our sacred arts curriculum. We have done this using a variety of art forms including writing, storytelling, movement, and visual arts. Again, we require a course in Sacred Arts as part of our ordination programs. In perhaps our most unusual art form we have engaged in teaching text through circus arts. This process of embodying the text, rather than only reading and analyzing it, has led to remarkable insights and growth among our students. While we may be the only rabbinical and cantorial school to have set up a tightwire in our *beit midrash* (study hall), or to have taken our students to a trapeze gym, these students will never read the texts examined through this methodology the same way again. While our students are generally eager to study in traditional ways as well, they are now prepared to use a fuller variety of approaches to help reach those for whom, perhaps, sitting around the table is not the preferred mode of study.

I also must share the joy with which we approach the publication of this present volume. AJR was founded in 1956 on the principle of *klal yisrael* and pluralism. At the height of denominationalism, our founders already knew that the Jewish community needs to have institutions and communities that lovingly include all forms of Jewish life and needs to have Jews who commit themselves to living lives that cherish diversity. In the United States, however, we were very much alone in these views. The current book shows how far ahead of their time our founders were, and we happily embrace this new Jewish world that understands the value of pluralistic Jewish life.

Part 2

Philosophies

The Substance of Jewish Denominations: Judaism Rooted in the Soul
Mordecai Finley

In the modern period, ever since the rise of Reform Judaism in the early nineteenth century, denominations have formed around theories of the commandments—which commandments we are obligated to observe and why. A given Jew might be more drawn toward, for example, Maimonidean or Kabbalistic thought; but what typically makes that Jew denominational is affiliation with a movement that has made a claim about *halakhic* (legal) obligation.

Theories of *halakhic* obligation themselves are rooted in ideas regarding the covenant between God and the people of Israel. The idea of "covenant" (*brit* in Hebrew), means that, at its core, Judaism is a religious tradition of obligations. If one is part of this covenant, one is obligated. To use the traditional terminology, one lives under the Yoke of the Commandments (*ol ha-mitzvot*). The different religious denominations in Judaism (Orthodox, Conservative, Reform, Reconstructionist, etc.) may differ in their understandings of God and what is required of us, but every religious movement would agree that Judaism is, minimally, a religion of duty.

Traditionally, the Jewish covenant with God has two main dimensions. One dimension is ethics, obligations that govern relationships between one person and another: "commandments between a person and one's fellow" (*mitzvot bein adam le-chavero*). The other dimension is practices that link us to the Divine: "commandments between a person and *Ha-Makom*," a rabbinic word for God that literally means "the Place" (*mitzvot bein adam la-makom*).

The practices that link us to the Divine have two aspects. The first is the inner life dimension (prayer, contemplation, meditation, and so forth). Also called *Chovot Ha-Levavot*, "Duties of the Heart," these practices have no overtly, observable dimension that indicates the fulfillment of the mitzvah. For example, a person might be holding a prayer book and mouthing the words, but from that we cannot deduce that the person is praying with intentionality.

The other traditions of *mitzvot* that link us to the Divine are the observable, behavioral ritual observances, such as those connected to Shabbat and holidays, keeping kosher, purity laws, wearing *tefillin* (phylacteries) and *tallit* (prayer shawl), etc.

If I am correct in stating that, in general, denominations are clustered mostly around degrees of observance or non-observance of the ritual, observable dimension, then nondenominational Judaism should focus on the inner life dimensions—the dimension that all denominations share, at least theoretically. In other words, in order to develop a concept of nondenominational Judaism, we have to engage in a system of thought that puts aside any *halakhic* considerations, and ask what ideas subsist foundationally beneath any theory of religious Judaism—putting aside for now non-religious theories of Judaism.

In thinking about a Judaism that transcends denominations, let's start with a brief presentation of a biblical theory of the human being, a philosophic anthropology that transcends religions in general.

The first step of the biblical philosophic anthropology being presented here is reflected in two passages in Genesis. In Genesis 1:26–27, *adam* (man/human) is created by the word of the Divine, male and female, in the Divine image and likeness. In Genesis 2:7, *adam* is shaped (*yitzer*) by the Divine, and then animated by a divine breath of life (*nishmat chayim*), and *adam* becomes a living being (*nefesh chaya*).

While a close study would reveal significantly different philosophic and religious implications of these two sources, for our purposes they present a complementary concept: the human has a divine dimension and is endowed with a divinely gifted spirit.

The second step in the brief biblical philosophic anthropology presented here is found in three main sources. In the first source, Genesis 6:5-6, we witness a Divine reflection and disappointment in the destructive dimension of the human being. The verse warrants full translation here: "Adonai saw that the wickedness of the human being was great upon the earth, and that every *yetzer* ["shape"—note the connection with Genesis 2:7, cited above] of thoughts of his *lev* are all bad, all day long, and [God] was sad to his *lev*."

Source two, from Genesis 8:21, second half of the verse, depicts God's reflecting after the great Flood. In this verse, God decides never to curse the earth again because of *adam*, and also gives the reasoning: "And Adonai said to his *lev*, 'I shall not continue anymore to curse the ground because of the human being, because the *yetzer* of the *lev* of the human being is bad from his youth.'"

The third source in this brief presentation of a biblical philosophic anthropology is from the book of Numbers, after the incident with spies (Num. 13–14), followed by the incident of the wood collector (Num. 15:3–26). In Numbers 15:37–41, we have the commandment to wear the fringes on four-cornered garments, followed by its reasoning: "And you shall not follow after your *lev* nor your eyes, after which you go astray."

One notes, of course, that the word *lev* is common in all these verses. We have left this word untranslated, as its usual translation, "heart," is rather misleading. In English, the metaphoric use of the word "heart" often connotes the seat of moral sentiments, human depth, etc. In English, we are often bidden to "follow the heart." We are sometimes reminded to "get out of our heads and into our hearts." In the Bible, however, we are explicitly commanded *not* to follow our hearts. In Genesis 6:5, we are told that the shape (*yetzer*) of thoughts of the human *lev* are all bad, all day long, a view repeated in Genesis 8:21. It would, then, be better to re-translate the word "*lev*." I prefer the term "ego-self" and further define this term as the unconscious but moldable part of the inner life characterized by patterns of thoughts, feelings, emotions, images, imagination, sensations, intuitions, drives, and impulses. The *yetzer ha-ra* is found in the ego-self. Unaided, the ego-self (*lev*), is guided by the impulses and desires, and therefore the thought and feelings, of the *yetzer*. However, when linked to guide by the world of *neshama*, the higher self, as it were, the ego-self can be transformed into an abode of Divinely shaped values.

If we redefine the word *lev* as above, then we can also retranslate the term *yetzer ha-ra*, usually translated as "the evil urge." *Yetzer*, as we have seen, is from the Hebrew word root that means to "shape" or "form." The *yetzer ha-ra*, then, is better translated as "a formation toward destructiveness," a forming that occurs in the *lev*, the ego-self.

With these verses in mind, we can present a brief biblical philosophic anthropology. The human being is created in the Divine image and likeness and endowed with a Divine spirit. The human being is also characterized by a shaping toward destructiveness. The essential problem of the human condition is that we are dual—like the Divine, but by our nature, bent on destructiveness.

The *lev* of the human is untrustworthy in its natural state. We humans are, however, teachable. The shape of the human ego-self, the *heart* of the human being (with the original Hebrew meaning in mind), can be transformed. It is the project of inner-life Judaism, the spiritual side, to transform the human being.

In summary, this biblical philosophic anthropology, which applies to all human beings, subsists beneath every evolutionary phase of Judaism, through biblical and rabbinic to the modern period. Judaism, whatever else it might be, is a way of thinking that is rooted in the idea that all human beings, including those in the covenant between God and Israel, are created by God in God's image and likeness, and that human beings are endowed with spirit—the breath of the Divine. All human beings, Israelites included, are also characterized by their flawed hearts. Whatever else our purpose in life might be, one great purpose is to have the heart shaped by the spirit.

For the sake of convenience, we'll refer to this inner-life dimension of Judaism as Jewish spirituality—a thought rooted in the idea that we are endowed with a *neshama*—a divine spirit, the breath of the divine. This term, spirituality, is so used and perhaps overused that it will require some specific attention. I am not claiming here that my approach toward the term is a normative one; my approach is rather a heuristic one. I want to think about the term as briefly and carefully as I can, and hopefully invite response and discourse in discussing nondenominational Judaism.

I say "think about" spirituality and not "define" the term because "spiritual" is one of those words that defines a root idea, concept or activity. For example, when you try to define the word "good," in the moral aspect, you end up reducing it to other words: "excellent in the ethical sense," or providing synonyms such as "upright." You end up having to define "ethical," "moral," and "upright," and soon find that you are back to using "good." To the student of language and meaning, this circularity means that we have discovered a root term. Speakers of a language know how to use the term because the word describes something core about our experience as human beings. Knowing how to use the word, however, does not mean we can easily come up with a good (in the nonmoral sense) definition that does not circle back on other related terms.

Here is one way I have worked with a root term such as "spiritual." In a room of people who speak English well, I first ask, *Who can define 'spiritual'?* The room is quiet. Then I ask, *What associations do you have with the word "spiritual"? What describes you when you feel spiritual? Think of a person you know, a character in a book or movie, whom you would describe as spiritual—what qualities make them so?*

Here is what I find: in a room of people, none of whom can define "spiritual"—all of them can use the word, and use it well, eloquently, and instructively. They say: centered, transcendent, strong, wise, compassionate, knowing, loving, courageous, principled, connected to God, deep, rooted, aware, soulful, disciplined, and so forth. Upon hearing this multiplicity of meanings, I ask the group: *Are there any terms here that are questionable?* Most of the time, people agree to keep all the terms.

I point out apparent contradictions: compassionate and principled, strong and loving, centered and transcendent, and so forth. I am quickly told, sometimes quite eloquently, that these apparent contradictions are just surface contradictions—a deeper logic ties them together.

I have come to teach that "spirituality" connotes and evokes a constellation of virtues, qualities, characteristics, and traits that are valuable in and of themselves. This means they are not valuable because they lead to something else. The constellation of virtues that describe "spiritual" are inherently of value, axiological, for a well-lived life.

In general, my students have known what spirituality means, even if they have not thought about it much nor can define it. Once students of spirituality invest the time in drawing out the term's meaning, they know they should become it—*be* spiritual. Like any value, its meaning is its claim on us. In other words, spirituality has inherent, not utilitarian value. Once you think about being wise, loving, principled, compassionate, morally strong, etc., you know that these words exert a kind of force in our thinking. We know we ought to strive to become and exemplify those words. At its deepest, spirituality is "commanded."

Since the term "spirituality" is core to my understanding of nondenominational Judaism (Jewish religious thought that sidesteps issues of *halakhic* ritual obligation), I want to discuss the term a bit more schematically, using the vertical metaphor of a ladder.

At every level of the ladder described below, we have to ask what differentiates Jewish spirituality from spiritual experience in general. Here I am making a normative claim: authentic Jewish spirituality requires immersion in, at a minimum, Jewish texts and the symbols, images, metaphors, and narratives contained therein. One can be a literate and observant Jew, but not one who has deep spiritual experiences shaped by that literacy and observance. One can also be a Jew who engages in social justice activism, for example, but, by the same token, not have spiritual experiences that can be described as "Jewish," absent an immersion in the language of Jewish texts.

At the highest end, we use the term "spiritual" to describe a kind of experience. At its deepest, a spiritual experience can be described as mystical: the experience of a realm that is wholly other to our normal, mundane existence. From a religious perspective, mystical experience can be understood as being brought into an overwhelming experience of God. To put a finer point on this idea: a Jew might believe that there is a God who commands *halakhic* observance or engagement in social justice efforts. Believing that there is a God is categorically different from having a profound experience of being brought into the presence of the Divine. Mystical experience of God does not respect denominational boundaries. Across the denominational board, mystical experience is an equal opportunity transformational experience.

A biblical text that might suggest this sort of mystical experience is Psalm 104:1–2, used in Jewish prayer as the meditation before donning the *tallit*:

> Oh, my soul—you bless God!
> [The soul says,] "Adonai Elohai, you are immense!
> You have adorned Yourself with majesty and splendor;

clothed in light like a garment,
stretching out the heavens like a canvas."
[my translation]

When we allow the soul to speak, it knows immediately of the greatness of God. Then the speaking soul shares a startling image—light is the garment of God. When we see light, we see the majestic, splendiferous garment of God, and therefore the hiddenness of the Divine. When we see the heavens, we see the canvas of Divine creation. Imagining that light reveals an image and likeness of God, contours of the Divine, hidden from view, can draw us into a mystical apprehension of the ineffable "shape of God"—a shape revealed by light.

A level down from the mystical experience is the experience of the love and grace of God. Using the prayer book's meditation on being wrapped in the *tallit* after putting it on, we find Psalm 36:8–11:

How precious is your lovingkindness, oh God.
Humanity seeks refuge in the shadow of Your wings.
They are sated with the abundance of Your abode
and You give drink from the brook of your delight.
For with you is the source [wellspring] of life,
In your light, we see light.
Draw your lovingkindness to those who know You
And Your righteousness to the upright of heart [*lev*].

This verse from Psalms moves from the mystical to the spiritual aspect of God's love. In a moment of stunning synesthesia, the spiritual seeker drinks of God's presence and sees the fountain of life. This verse then takes us from spiritual experience (the knowers of God) to an ethical charge: God's righteousness is drawn to the upright of heart—those who shape their ego-selves toward righteousness.

The term used here—*yodekha*, "those who know You"—can serve as a key phrase for the spiritual experience of God. A knower of God does not simply accept the fact of God's existence but knows God in the manner suggested here—as drinking abundance of the Divine abode, as seeing the fountain of life, as having been given sight by seeing God's light, as experiencing God's lovingkindness and being drawn toward God's righteousness.

A step down the ladder away from deep spiritual experience is the realm of ethics—the demand that ego-self be shaped by a commitment to righteousness. A text that can serve as a guide here might be Psalm 15:

> Who may sojourn in Your tent, oh God?
> Who may dwell upon Your holy mountain?
> One who walks unblemished.
> One who performs righteousness and speaks the
> truth in his heart [*lev*]
> One who does not slander and does no evil to his
> fellow...

Texts on Jewish ethics and character abound in the Bible, rabbinic literature, and Mussar literature; there is no need to duplicate those texts here. Suffice it to say that a key part of Jewish spirituality is the conscious shaping of the ego-self according to the contours of righteousness. I want to stress here that acting according to Jewish values has to be internalized into character transformation, so that we not only *do* good, but *become* good.

When we move into traditional practices that have *halakhic* dimensions, such as *tefillah* (prayer) and Sabbath and holiday observances, we again stress the focus on inner experience, not the fulfillment of the behavioral side of the commandment. For example, in *tefillah*, spiritual transformation would privilege *kavanah*, spiritual intention, over *keva*, the standard prayer liturgy. Such an emphasis on *kavanah* might seem to side with the progressive movements in Judaism as opposed to the more traditional, but great caution is urged here to avoid facile distinctions. Many people can recall an abbreviated Reform prayer service, with responsive readings in English that feel anything but filled with *kavanah*. In fact, people often experience Reform prayer services as desiccated and rote, while noting the spiritual fervor of an Orthodox service. Any denomination can slide into a dried out, routinized "service of the heart" barely worthy of the name, that leaves the ego-self untouched. Conversely, any denomination can be committed to prayer services filled with opportunities for spiritual experience in a shared place and time, with a shared liturgy.

This same focus on fostering spiritual experience—the experience of God and the conscious transformation of the ego-self—can apply to how we study Torah and how we celebrate Shabbat and holidays. This brief chapter is not the place for a full presentation of how to cultivate, for example, *tefillah*, Torah study, and Shabbat and Mo'ed observance as spiritual experiences. My focus here is to emphasize that such a focus and study transcend any denominational concern. Whatever *halakhic* considerations shape our communities, we should all make use of our own versions of Jewish practice to combat the *yetzer ha-ra* and bring the spirit of the Divine into our hearts, transforming ourselves, those around us, and perhaps in ways that we can't fully articulate, changing our world and even touching the heart of God.

Masechet BB – Beyond Binaries
Adam Chalom

A member of my congregation had a cousin facing a relapse of breast cancer. The member asked whether, if she found out her cousin's Hebrew name, I would be willing to say some prayers. I replied, "I have a different idea. Why don't you get me her phone number, and I'll call her? Maybe we'll talk about her condition and she'll feel better, or we'll talk about something totally different to take her mind off what she's facing. Either way, she will know that someone cares." Sending words out into the universe may or may not have any impact, but we know that personal connection and a positive attitude can have positive effects on recovery. Even if the case is terminal, we can talk about how best to use her remaining days to have a lasting impact on her family, and deeper meaning in her goodbyes.

Any approach to Jewish inclusion for the twenty-first century must create space for Jews who focus on this life, this world, and a secular human experience. This may mean pushing the envelope on the meanings of words like sacred and profane, or belief and meaning, or even Judaism itself. The joy and the challenge of contemporary Jewish life is that we often meet and work with and serve individuals who have different beliefs from ours—and a substantial portion of the American Jewish community is some kind of secular. According to Pew's 2013 study "A Portrait of Jewish Americans," 22% of all American Jews and 32% of Jewish Millennials say they are Jewish but not religious. They are secular in both belief and behavior: 23% "do not believe in a god or universal spirit" (compared to 7% of the general U.S. population), and 22% never attend Jewish religious services, not even High Holidays.[1] Of course, those three groups are not all the same people—some "non-believers" or the "non-religious" do attend synagogue from time to time, and some of the "non-religious" believe in a god or universal spirit. In whatever way they are secularized, some of

---

[1] Pew Research Center, "A Portrait of Jewish Americans," October 1, 2013, https://www.pewforum.org/wp-content/uploads/sites/7/2013/10/jewish-american-full-report-for-web.pdf

these Jews will find their way to the offices or email inboxes of every variety of twenty-first-century rabbi and Jewish community. Serving them requires understanding how they find meaning in Judaism and life in general.

Secular Humanistic Judaism has been serving these Jews and their families for over fifty years. We are the paradox, beyond the binary, of secular congregations: religious by structure—Shabbat and holiday services, rabbis, the big questions we answer, the human needs we meet—and secular by belief. While empowering individual choice, we share a belief in the importance of human action, power, knowledge, and responsibility. That positive focus means a range of theological opinions can be comfortable in our tent—everything from hard-core atheists to agnostics to deists who believe in something before the Big Bang to some who believe in something beyond knowing. If you believe in a god who intervenes in the world, writes a Torah, cares what you eat or wear or whom you love, wants to be praised and petitioned and blessed, then you have many Jewish options. We provide community that celebrates Jewish culture in a secular key.

Mishnah Aleph – Beyond Binaries – Kodesh V'khol

In the traditional Havdalah blessing, there are clear distinctions: *bein kodesh l'khol, bein or l'khoshekh, bein Yisrael l'amim, bein yom hashvi'i l'sheishet y'mei ha-ma'aseh*—between light and darkness, Israel and the nations, the seventh day and the six days of work, and between sacred and "profane/mundane/secular." In graduate school, I once tried to claim that the use of *khol*, the basis for the modern Hebrew term for secular "*khiloni*," meant that rabbinic Judaism had a place for secularism, or at least for secular experience. A professor corrected me: before modern times, anything "*khol*" was *not* secular or even "profane" as we understand those words today. A pious and minimally educated Jew of those days would have experienced what we call religion *all the time* on a "profane" day: *kashrut* (dietary laws) and blessings and prayers from the time they rose to the time they lay down, as they walked on their way, or passed the doorposts of their house. After all, days of *khol ha-mo'ed* (intermediate festival days) in the middle of Passover or Sukkot are not secular festivals. Perhaps *khol* is better translated "ordinary," but the ordinary can also be suffused with special meaning.

Contemporary liturgist Marcia Falk has a different take on Havdalah, on distinctions, on sacred and mundane, that I find more meaningful than the traditional *mavdil* blessing:

> Let us distinguish parts within the whole and bless their differences.
>
> Like the Sabbath and the six days of creation, may our lives be made whole through relation.
>
> As rest makes the Sabbath precious, may our work give meaning to the week.
>
> Let us separate the Sabbath from other days of the week, seeking holiness in each.[2]

Here there are distinctions, but they are not oppositions like light and dark or Israel and the other 99.8% of humanity. Parts within the whole have a shared context in the human heart. Whether one believes in a cosmic unity of creation, or instead prefers a holistic approach to the human experience, or any variation beyond those alternatives—all of us experience the world and make meaning out of it. And we do this all the time, not just in sacred time and sacred modes of thought and emotion.

Mishnah Bet – Beyond Binaries – Belief and Non-Belief

I am a believer, but I am not a person of faith. I once took a phone survey near an election, and I was amused by the demographic questions they asked. Has the clergy in your congregation spoken on political issues recently? I had to think, "Did I?" How often do you attend religious services? "All the time." How often do you pray? "Never." As a Humanistic Jew, I was raised to believe and I still believe in human rights and dignity, in human freedom and in human potential. I believe that human knowledge can and has transformed the world, for good and for evil: we live longer and better, and can die more horribly, than ever. I believe that we have responsibilities to

---

[2] Marcia Falk, *The Book of Blessings: New Jewish Prayers for Daily Life, the Sabbath, and the New Moon Festival* (Boston, MA: Beacon, 1999), 318.

each other, and that everyone has the right to live their truths, their identities, their values, their loving partnerships in full joy and at full volume. I believe that human morality, evolved for group survival and refined by generations of thought and experience, is the only conscious and active force working in this world to reward the good, to punish evil, to birth justice, and to meet human needs. And I believe that my Judaism is most meaningful when it reflects my values through an expression of my Jewish inheritance of literature, law, custom, and ceremony.

Why do human beings believe things much less provable than gravity? For many reasons: we like to think our beliefs are mostly because of evidence and experience, but emotion and bias and personal interest and human needs play a much larger role than we like to admit.[3] People of faith in the conventional sense seem to keep looking for and pointing to evidence when it supports their case, while so-called "non-believers" can be very dogmatic about their doubts. I once saw an amusing bumper sticker which said, "militant agnostic: I don't know and neither do you!"

I take my epistemological humility seriously: my Humanistic Judaism is mine. It provides explanation and meaning and inspiration to me; I do not assume you must agree with me for us to break bread together, or to work together, or celebrate Jewish life together.

Rabbinic thought says there are seventy faces to the Torah, or that it was revealed differently to the 600,000 who received it (unfortunately, they only counted men, to their shame and to our responsibility for *tikkun* [repair]). We interpret with "*davar akher*," a new interpretation that co-exists with what came before and what is yet to come. We study legal discussions across centuries, adding commentaries and debating in *chevruta* (partnership). "The Human Experience" can be amazingly varied: men and women and beyond the binary, affluent and struggling, healthy and challenged, too long and too short. Why should we assume there is *one* meaning of life, *one* source for personal meaning, *one* approach to making sense of it all that will answer

---

[3] See Jonathan Haidt, *The Righteous Mind: Why Good People Are Divided by Politics and Religion* (New York: Vintage Books/Random House, 2013), Part I: "Intuitions Come First, Strategic Reasoning Second."

everyone's questions every time for their entire life?

Mishnah Gimmel – Beyond Binaries – Secular and Spiritual

Aware that beauty enriches our lives, evokes the most powerful emotions, and inspires the noblest ambitions—aware, that is, that beauty causes the spirit to soar—we naturally wish to cultivate beauty and the appreciation of beauty....It is clear that, absent belief in God, you are nevertheless a spiritual person. Unless you have no use for music, literature, drama, or dance, unless you are oblivious to the genius of Shakespeare and Chopin and the talent of Michael Jordan, unless you are indifferent to the majesty of a mountain range or the spectacle of a starry sky. It is clear that your spirituality derives entirely from within you. It is clear that each of us imposes our notions of beauty upon mountains and men. That is our greatness.

– Rabbi Daniel Friedman[4]

Where does a secular person find inspiration and meaning in life? Recall Marcia Falk's *havdalah*: meaning is not only to be found in the "sacred," be that conventionally defined by *mitzvot* (commandments) and prayers, or creatively understood as that which we deem most important; the mundane, the profane, the secular, the ordinary of everyday life have their moments too. I do not mean that every moment is a miracle—every moment is a *moment*, an opportunity we get to enjoy or use or waste or breathe or simply be in the world, in love, in our family, in dialogue with our tradition or with just one other person.

And we are a meaning-making species. Yuval Noah Harari's fascinating journey through the human experience, *Sapiens*, points out that our explosions in agriculture and technology and society began at the same time we mastered imagination: money and nationality

---

[4] Daniel Friedman, "Art and Nature: Beauty and Spirituality," in *Secular Spirituality: Passionate Search for a Rational Judaism*, ed. M. Bonnie Cousens (Farmington Hills, MI: IISHJ/Milan, 2003), 108.

and human rights, and perhaps even religion, are creative steps to add meaning to what we physically experience.[5] Lightning strikes, or a child dies, or we find a tree full of fruit. It is we who believe that Zeus punishes or that sins are visited on the third and fourth generation of those who reject a god or that it is a miraculous tree of life.

Here are some examples of moments a secular Jew might find meaningful, moments that support their beliefs and give them strength to persevere through struggles and doubts. Of course, religious people may also experience these as meaningful even if their meaning-making differs. In Israel, secular Jewishness was once compared to an empty cart, which should yield when facing the full cart of Orthodoxy. The truth is that our cart is also full, because we meet human needs in ways that are consistent with our philosophical Humanism.[6]

Connecting with religious heritage: This could be using the Hanukkah menorah one's great-grandfather brought to America from Europe, or hearing the intentionally anachronistic sound of a *shofar* (ram's horn) on Rosh Hashanah—a trumpet wouldn't be the same. Seeing one's grandchildren married under a *chuppah* (canopy) and breaking a glass. These experiences transcend time and individuality to help one feel connected to both the past and the future. In 1911, Chaim Zhitlowsky, a Yiddishist secularist, wrote:

> Religious images, myths and ceremonies become precious to us not because we believe in their divine origin, but because our spirit is moved by their human beauty. They evoke in us such poetic feelings and thoughts that we consider them humanistic sanctities.[7]

---

[5] Yuval Noah Harari, *Sapiens: A Brief History of Humankind* (New York: Harper, 2015).

[6] See Alain de Botton, *Religion for Atheists: A Non-believer's Guide to the Uses of Religion* (New York: Pantheon, 2012).

[7] Haim Zhitlovsky, "The National Poetic Rebirth of the Jewish People," trans. Max Rosenfeld, in *Judaism in a Secular Age: An Anthology of Secular Humanistic Jewish Thought*, ed. Renee Kogel and Zev Katz (Jersey City, NJ: Ktav, 1995), 93.

As human rather than divine creations, the feeling of cultural continuity evoked by a symbol combined with the family continuity of heirlooms and the communal solidarity of collective celebration can uplift human spirit in a secular key, and thus be a deeply meaningful moment.

Personal Meditation: This could be a few moments at the beginning of a *Kabbalat Shabbat* celebration before lighting candles, or thirty minutes of silence to start one's day alone, or a weekend retreat with strangers. Judaism is a very verbal culture, but sometimes the right response, the right way to find meaning and offer meaning, is silence. We fall into the trap that meaning is about content, defining and describing and then prescribing action; often meaning is about feeling and experiencing, with analysis to follow. *Maybe*. Meditation provides meaning because it creates an opportunity for us to feel grounded, less focused on our busy and active minds and more in tune with our emotions, and even our physical bodies.

The Natural World: Watching a nature special on great apes, I once thought, "How human they are behaving," until I realized that in fact we are behaving like them. Long walks in nature, paying attention to the changing seasons, standing in silence before awe-inspiring views—all these experiences uplift the human spirit. We are part of the natural world, and whether it is the magnificence of natural wonders or fascinating details of the sub-atomic, we can be inspired to be part of this chain of life and existence.[8] All the more reason to preserve and protect it, and to experience it while we can. The famous evolutionary biologist (and atheist) Richard Dawkins was asked how an atheist can get up in the morning without hope of an afterlife. His reply: that's *why* I get up in the morning! This is my only opportunity!

Beauty and Culture: Just as the natural world can astonish and inspire, so too can human creations in culture and the arts. Think of an astonishingly beautiful poem, or a painting that captures the

---

[8] The short documentary *Powers of Ten: A Film Dealing with the Relative Size of Things in the Universe and the Effect of Adding Another Zero* (Pyramid Films, 1977) is a wonderful demonstration in both directions: https://www.youtube.com/watch?v=0fKBhvDjuy0

essence of human loneliness. A movie scene that stays with you for the rest of your life. An aria that brings tears to your eyes, even if you have no idea what it means. I remember finishing books and wishing I could read them again for the first time. I find meaning through beauty because great art expresses deep truths about human experience and wisdom for the human condition. The connection of minds and hearts across generations in an artistic encounter means the artist and I share something that transcends time and death.

History and Roots: My first visit to the Western Wall was meaningful, but not because I was any closer to God or the Holy of Holies or the Temple, nor because I left a written prayer I hoped would be answered. It was when I touched the stones and found they were smooth: worn smooth from the generations of hands of my people that had touched them; it was like touching their hands through time and space. Go to the cave paintings in Lascaux and see the image of a human hand from 17,000 years ago. Or the birth of your child, or the first time you hear your partner's laugh from your child's lips. In all these moments, we understand both intellectually and emotionally that we are part of something larger than ourselves. That natural transcendence, from natural world or human roots, gives us perspective on our own issues—like the famous poster of the Milky Way galaxy with an arrow pointing to a small dot with the words "you are here." It is also a reminder of the wisdom of Psalms 133:1: *Hinei ma tov*—how good and pleasant for family to live together.

Ethics, Activism, and Human Connection: Many people find secular meaning by living out their values in the world, be it in specific ethical situations or in working for broader moral causes of justice, compassion, or whatever one deems to be *tikkun olam*. It doesn't need to be a global socialist revolution, as secular Yiddishists hoped for and worked for a century ago, to feel like one is making a tangible difference in the course of human existence. And helping others can also help us. A couple facing financial challenges went to their rabbi for advice, and she suggested that they give a small amount of *tzedakah* (charity) each week. Though they were initially dubious, they found that these small donations helped them feel better because they had the power to help others. Interpersonal connections, whether in a relationship of support and assistance, a romantic connection, a deep personal bond, a caring community, or advocacy and allyship—none of these require theology or supernaturalism to be personally transformative and to give a sense of meaning and purpose to one's life.

These are some of the ways that Humanistic beliefs and values can inform moments of meaning, and moments of meaning inspire Humanistic beliefs.

> When we feel insignificant in the midst of a vast and overwhelming universe but feel significant as a part of a single nature evolving through the ages; when we feel insignificant as a lonely and mortal individual but feel significant as part of a centuries long chain of family love; when we see ourselves as powerless fighting the forces of evil alone but see ourselves as powerful when joined together with others in a movement of political idealism—we experience the wonder of natural transcendence.
>
> – Rabbi Sherwin Wine[9]

These are wells of inspiration I turn to when I need clarity or calm or rejuvenation, which today, eighteen years after my own rabbinic ordination, I need just as much if not more.

Mishnah Dalet – Beyond Binaries – The Creator and the Created

We are indeed meaning-makers, and there are many faces and facets of the human and Jewish pursuit of meaning. For secular and Humanistic Jews, that sense of meaning does not spring from beyond this world, a revelation of ultimate truth. It comes, rather, from the human condition in all of its glorious limitations. We Jews are created by Jewish culture and tradition, and we create the Jewish culture and tradition that creates us from year to year, from season to season, from generation to generation. *Baruch atah Yisrael, notein ha-Torah—*

---

[9] Sherwin Wine, "Secular Spirituality," in *Secular Spirituality: Passionate Search for a Rational Judaism*, ed. M. Bonnie Cousens (Farmington Hills, MI: IISHJ/Milan, 2003), 181.

Blessed are you Israel, who gives the Torah. Chaim Zhitlowsky said it beautifully:

> Like poetry and philosophy, religion is an everlasting branch on the tree of human culture. Its leaves may wither and fall, but others sprout in their place. The source of religion is an eternal wellspring—the yearning of the human soul for a better and more beautiful world. As Ludwig Feuerbach put it: "God is a tear that human beings weep over their own destiny." And the wellsprings of such tears will never dry up.[10]

---

[10] Haim Zhitlovsky, "Death and Rebirth of Gods and Religion," trans. Max Rosenfeld, in *Judaism in a Secular Age: An Anthology of Secular Humanistic Jewish Thought*, ed. Renee Kogel and Zev Katz (Jersey City, NJ: Ktav, 1995), 93.

Will the Real Jewish Heretic Please Stand Up
Rochelle Robins

Radical Acceptance

In order for the Jewish people to live as fully united as possible, just as in any other relationship, reshaping or changing an individual or group cannot be the goal. When we risk radical acceptance of ourselves and others—and resolve to stay in and improve relationship amidst difference—tangible inner, interpersonal, and societal transformation can occur. My dream is that Judaism can serve as a template for a "place in the world where people can engage in one another's differences in a way that is redemptive, full of hope and possibility. Not this 'In order to love you, I must make you something else.' That's what domination is all about, that in order to be close to you, I must possess you, remake and recast you."[1] While this bell hooks quote focuses on the ideas of intersectionality, feminism, social justice, activism, and anti-racism, in my mind it is closely connected to my notion of *l'taken olam b'malkhut shaddai*—repairing the world and pouring ourselves into "the interconnectedness of all life."[2]

All too often, Jews are attempting to recast one another to fit a single story of truth, identity, and experience. Survival and thriving are reliant on recasting ourselves with innovation and creativity—tending to the actual needs of time's currents. There are multiple stories of recasting and reshaping that have led us to where we are today. When recasting and reshaping the Jewish people is reliant on a single story, the narrative becomes one-sided and untrue. The truth of Judaism exists in its multiplicity and evolutionary cycles. My dream of an inclusive "non-reshaping of the other" Judaism is one in which we sharpen our knowledge, practice, ethics, and moral intuitions

---

[1] bell hooks, *Reel to Real: Race, Sex, and Class at the Movies* (New York: Psychology, 1996), 122. hooks prefaced this comment with, "I want there to be a place in this world…"

[2] Tiferet Berenbaum, *"Aleinu*: A Call to Divine Service," *My Jewish Learning*, https://www.myjewishlearning.com/article/aleinu-a-call-to-divine-service/

through compassion for and curiosity of what is important to one another—perhaps even or especially what may seem unpalatable to us.

Although there is a vast number of positive and meaningful exchanges within and between us, we are living with unnecessary and unfounded hegemonies in the Jewish world, where individuals and communities question the authenticity of other individuals and communities. Yet it is precisely this diversity that has upheld our existence. Author bell hooks also says, "People with healthy esteem do not need to create pretend identities."[3] Positive identities are built in response to and in relationship with others, not in reaction to others. There is a challenge in progressive Jewish movements to allow conversation in discord. This is where those who embrace pluralist and the most contemporary transdenominational[4] approaches have the opportunity to show courage and strength. Identity isn't inherently threatened by other beliefs, views, and opinions—even if those opinions directly oppose our stance. Identity becomes stronger and more positive through connecting with others who live in different realities. We are challenged to strengthen our abilities to accept and engage in difficult conversations with other kinds of Jews.

Rav Kook claimed that revelation didn't discontinue at Mount Sinai. Revelation occurs in human interactions within the context of the stories and relationships that we build throughout history. He claimed that history itself is a conversation with God.[5] While it may seem antithetical to mention a contemporary transdenominational egalitarian dream in the same breath as Rav Kook, who didn't even support women's suffrage, both viewpoints illustrate evolving thought related to the societal concerns and conditions of their times. If we were to imagine a syncretic dialogue—combining different beliefs

---

[3] bell hooks, *Rock My Soul: Black People and Self-Esteem* (New York: Simon and Schuster, 2003), 92.

[4] While the word *transdenominational* is readily used and is perhaps the ultimate choice to express the phenomenon of Jews of all backgrounds uniting, the word *denomination* originated to mark divisions within the Christian world beginning in seventeenth-century Europe. Although the term transdenominationalism deserves further discussion, it essentially indicates and describes Jewish communities coming together.

[5] One of the many publications that explains and explores Rav Kook's view on continuing revelation is Ben Zion Bokser, ed., *The Essential Writings of Rabbi Abraham Isaac Kook* (Teaneck, NJ: Ben Yehuda Press, 2008).

within a single conversation—between Rav Kook and someone like myself, it would be rich and varied. Jewish feminist scholar and theologian Rachel Adler explores the Jewish pedagogy and andragogy of *k'nai l'kha chaver*: "Acquire for yourself a companion." She quotes and translates *Avot d'Rabbi Natan* 8:

> *K'nai l'kha chaver*: This teaches that a person should set himself a companion, to eat with him, drink with him, study Bible with him, study Mishna with him, sleep with him, and reveal to him all his secrets, secrets of Torah and secrets of worldly things.[6]

Adler then writes:

> This rabbinic text describes a distinctively Jewish kind of intimacy: the study-companion relationship. The *chaverim* do not simply study Bible and Mishna; the very structure of their relationship and the nature of its boundaries present a Jewish model for the relation between the self and the other. In this relationship, people experience each other as whole, rather than as fragmented, beings. Companionship is simultaneously physical, emotional, intellectual, and spiritual. Self and other are not sharply separate here. To be *chaverim* is to be neither fused nor counterposed, but to be juxtaposed. The root CH-B-R means to join together at the boundaries.[7]

We are living at a time in which questions and conversations are narrowing rather than expanding. This creates less rather than more intimacy. The trans-Jewish movement seeks to maintain the multivocal and expansive conversation that characterizes core foundations of Jewish cultures and survival. This is an area of strength that we

---

[6] Rachel Adler, "A Question of Boundaries: Toward a Jewish Feminist Theology of Self and Others," *Tikkun* (May/June 1991).
[7] Ibid.

can offer and share both within and outside of the Jewish community.

Expanding Questions

An imaginary syncretic conversation with Rav Kook and a Jewish feminist theologian, such as Dr. Adler, or a real one with all living individuals from divergent schools of thought, would require expanding questions of curiosity and openness; it would require conversing without the triggers of threat or attempts to prove our positions through rhetorical questions. It would also require us to actually ask questions rather than set up our inquiries through statements of proof. Recently, following a presentation, I witnessed a rabbi from a non-mainstream Jewish movement being questioned by a group of faculty and students. While a number of the inquiries were presented with depth, others created an either/or atmosphere during the conversation—establishing a competition between schools of thought and challenging the potential gaps in the rabbi's position. Some questions are better than others. For instance, perhaps it would be more effective and respectful not to ask an atheist whether they see a dogma in their own position and instead ask the person why they believe their approach and belief system is important in an expanding Jewish view and world view. The first question creates competition. The second presents a stance of curiosity, compassion, and learning. Adler reminds us that a core motivation of Jewish philosophy, thought, text, and tradition is to promote intricate conversations where companionship and learning relies not on an impermeable self but on the interconnectedness and interdependency of human relationships.

Listening

The watchword of Jewish religious consciousness, the *Shema*, is focused on the essentiality of listening. Commentaries, articles, and books abound on the meaning of the *Shema* and the blessings that surround it.[8] Every year at the Academy for Jewish Religion California's graduation/ordination ceremony, the chaplaincy graduates hear these words: "You are commissioned and endorsed as an educated

---

[8] One of the many publications that explains and explores the *Shema* is Lisa Aiken, *The Hidden Beauty of the Shema* (New York: Judaica, 2004).

and skilled practitioner and spiritual leader, who listens and responds according to the values of our tradition. And how you respond is how you hear *Shema Yisrael*, 'Hear, O Israel,' in each and every given context. This is your practice, your art, your service, and your expertise."

These words serve as a mandate for each graduate, urging them to fulfill those expectations according to their individual skills and talents. The spiritual leader, and especially a trained chaplain, is responsible for hearing and listening to the struggles of our time—even when the struggles or sentiments presented are distasteful to the chaplain. The transdenominational Jew, the person who values relationships and discourse across the spectrum, is challenged to offer their listening and hearing, even as they are struggling to accept the content. In my imagination, I would listen to and hear the depth of Rav Kook and he would return the same courtesy to me to broaden our world views, even as our shoulders would feel heavy with the perception of the other's narrowness. It is my fantasy that within our diverse Jewish communities and practices, Jews can serve as an *or chadash al tzion tair*, a light among the nations, both inside and across our own communities of comfort. This is a progressive messianic vision that demands courage, responsibility, and presence for one another.

To Tell the Truth

To Tell the Truth, a game show that aired from 1956 to 1978, captured the attention of television viewers. Hollywood star panelists interviewed three contestants, all of whom claimed to possess something unique about their lives: an experience, a profession, or a bizarre and captivating oddity. Each contestant tried to convince the panelists that the story belonged to them. Two of them were actors and the other was the truth-teller. At the conclusion of the storytelling, each panelist would determine which of the contestants was the truth-teller and, by implication, who they believed to be imposters. After the panelist verdicts, the show host would ask, "Will the real so-and-so please stand up" (not as a question but as a command), at which time the real possessor of the experience was revealed. I imagine this show with my siblings and myself as the contestants. The question would be, "Will the real Jewish heretic please stand up," which is more entertaining and provocative than "Who is the most exemplary Jew among you?"

Stories and truth-telling become much more complex in real life. Unlike the original show, where there is one ultimate truth-teller, my version of it would demand that the panelists, along with the audience, engage the question in a manner that would expose the intricacies because we, the contestants, are all authentic. The "we" in my show would be my sister, my brother, and myself. The first, an Ultra-Orthodox settler of the West Bank; the second, someone who defines himself as an anthropological-cultural Jew who married into a Vietnamese Roman Catholic family and is raising his children in a Reform synagogue; and the third, a gay Reform ordained rabbi who has lived all over the map of Jewish thought, culture, and practice. The contestants are the children of a rabbi father who was raised within strict orthodoxy, served in Japan during WWII, rebelled against his Orthodox upbringing, and eventually dropped out of law school to enter the Reform rabbinate. Their mother was raised Conservative with degrees of spiritual and dietary flexibility. Both were children of immigrants and both were embracing of all peoples.

Fortunately, the question of who is exemplary and who represents heresy isn't a subject that my siblings and I engage; we respect one another and know what not to discuss in honor of *shalom*. The questions are, who crafts the questions and who sets the stage for the answers? The panelists and contestants would be watched by a broader public who may or may not be able to reach a consensus about the truth. In addition, much of the audience would be swayed by diminutive thinking and a lack of exposure. This happens not because minds and hearts are small, but because minds and hearts are cultivated to think and feel small. Most of us are products of this miniscule cultivation in the vast expanse of issues and life experiences to consider.

Authenticity

"Authentic" Judaism is as authentic as those living it. Our texts are filled with questions of authenticity. How does one know if a prophet is authentic?[9] Who were the authentic compilers and editors of the

---

[9] Sforno on Deuteronomy 18:13:1.

Talmud?[10] What is the real worth of diamonds?[11] When we search the canons of Jewish literature and sacred text throughout the ages, and the vast ocean of seemingly endless secondary literary sources, Jewish scholars wrestle with discussions of what comprises authentic Jewish existence. Today, questions arise, such as, is it possible for an intermarried couple to raise a Jewish family? Is honoring the dietary laws relegated to an Orthodox *hechsher* (rabbinical certification and approval)? Can one authentically espouse Jewish values and traditions within the LGBTQI+ communities? Can a Jewish individual married to a non-Jewish spouse become a rabbi, cantor, or Jewish chaplain? While these questions contain indicators of contemporary times, questions about how one engages customs, practices, and peoplehood aren't new at all. Questions about who belongs and who is forced to the margins are ancient if not pre-historical.

The often-stated notion that "traditional" Judaism or Orthodoxy is Judaism expressed in its original form denies the inherent evolutionary process that has accompanied the Jewish people's adaptation and survival throughout the ages. The Rambam, Maimonides himself— the man who is thought to be the most influential Jewish thinker of medieval times; the man who wrote the *Mishneh Torah* and codified and schematized the majority of Jewish law to make it more accessible to all; the man who today few Jews, from Orthodox to secular, would deny his righteous contributions to the Jewish people—was considered by many in his own time to be a heretic for seeing no conflict between Jewish thought and Aristotelian philosophy. For Maimonides, not only was there no conflict between Jewish and Greek philosophy, but they were inherently one and the same due to Aristotle's travels to the Land of Israel with Alexander the Great and studying with Jewish sages.[12] In addition, Maimonides, who resided in twelfth-century Islamic Spain, Morocco, and Egypt, was perhaps even more influenced by Islamic thought than Aristotelian ideas.

The word "heretics" or "heresies," *minim* in Hebrew, was origi-

---

[10] *Shulchan Arukh, Choshen Mishpat* 25:1. The text says that Ashi and Rabina were largely responsible for compiling and arranging the *halakhic*/legislative text.

[11] *Akeidat Yitzchak* 46:1.

[12] See Lewis Jacobs, *The Jewish Religion: A Companion* (New York: Oxford University Press, 1995).

nally associated with Jews who gravitated toward Greek philosophy. Similarly, the Greek-derived word, *apikoros*, which is found in the Talmud, refers to an individual who will not gain a place in the World to Come due to disrespecting the Talmudic sages through honoring philosophic ideas.[13] The word *apikoros* itself is thought to originate from the name of the Greek philosopher Epicurus, though this is never directly mentioned in the text. Given the Talmudic definition of heretic, Maimonides certainly met the criteria for heresy. Perhaps unsurprisingly, his own definition of the term *apikoros* differed from the Talmudic idea in that instead of relying on philosophy to gain heretical status, one must denounce and deny the idea of prophecy rather than philosophy.[14]

Prophecy

Prophecy, according to the teachings of Maimonides, is "an effluence that flows forth from God through the medium of the Active Intellect, first upon the rational faculty, and then upon the imaginative faculty."[15] Maimonides accentuated the idea of the active intellect in the transmission of revelation and prophetic vision without disputing the generally accepted notion that the destruction of the Temple and exile ended the formal biblical prophetic era. While the standard answer is that this era concluded with the Babylonian exile, according to Benjamin Sommer, scholars dispute whether the end of the prophetic era concluded with the destruction of the First or Second Temple.[16] Findings by scholars, such as Ephraim Urbach and David Greenspahn, convincingly argue that prophecy was robust during the Second Temple era and even the rabbinic period.[17]

Maimonides' accentuation of the importance of intellect supported his gravitation toward Jewish interpretations of Greek and Islamic

---

[13] Babylonian Talmud, *Seder Nezikin*, tractate *Sanhedrin* 99b.

[14] Maimonides, *Mishneh Torah, Hilchot Teshuvah* 3:6–8. The other categories of heresy are the refusal to accept the prophetic vision of Moses and the denial of God's knowledge of the actions of human beings.

[15] Alvin Jay Reines, *Maimonides and Abrabanel on Prophecy* (Cincinnati, OH: Hebrew Union College Press, 1970), www.jstor.org/stable/j.ctt19cc25q

[16] Benjamin D. Sommer, "Did Prophecy Cease? Evaluating a Reevaluation," *Journal of Biblical Literature* 115:1 (1996): 31.

[17] Ibid.

philosophical frameworks. It is indisputable that Greek and Islamic thought informed his Jewish intellect. He protected himself well in his reworking of the definition of heresy not to include his philosophical leanings. At what point did he himself lose his heretical status among the majority of *halakhic*, Jewish law-abiding communities? This process was evidently as slow as it was thorough. Over time, heretics can and frequently do become holy vessels for change.

Determining that Maimonides' own intellect protected him well isn't a slight. On the contrary, this is one aspect of the evolutionary cycle and adaptive process of Jewish life, culture, and practice to which we owe him and innumerable others credit. Maimonides was not living in isolation. He drew from the concepts, cultures, and people around him. We sharpen who we become through those around us. The idea of who we are may be a fantasy. Reality is richer than any label.

The Intellect and Prophetic Vision Continued

Maimonidean reliance on the intellect as the primary contributor to the continued act of revelation is one of the ways the Jewish stage was set to progress toward new thought and illumination. But this goes even farther back. If stagnancy were the trend at the time of the destruction of the Second Temple, and the rabbis of the Great Sanhedrin hadn't reformatted Jewish observance from the Temple cult to other liturgical and daily observances, Maimonides himself would not have retained enough Jewish, rabbinical, or practical context to influence the next steps on the path through his own intellect. Thus, it would seem that revelation and the evolution of the Jewish people is interminable.

The *Or HaChaim* states: "You should know that we have permission to explain the implication of the verses after careful study—even though our conclusions differ from the explanation of our Sages. That is because there are 70 faces to the Torah. There is no prohibition against differing from the words of our Sages except if it changes the *Halakha*."[18] Jewish expression has consistently valued a multiplicity of thoughts, ideas, and implications in its texts and cultures.

---

[18] Hayyim Ben Moshe Ibn Attar, *Or Hachaim*, Genesis 1:1:25.

Twentieth-century rabbi and educator Mordecai Kaplan's concept of Judaism as an evolving religious civilization captures a realistic view of the nature of tribal, societal, historical, and theological transformation throughout Israelite and Jewish existence.[19] An array of contributors, populations, polemics, and influences led to an evolutionary journey of what would become, and is still becoming, the Jewish people, identity, and experience. Innovation, adaptation, and evolution have led to the continual making and reshaping of Jewish life. There is no original Jewish people, yet all Jewish experience is connected to foundations and origins that are authentic.

Kaplan believed the progression of Jewish life is historically- and community-based, and not rooted in supernatural powers. He proposed that Jewish jurisprudence and practice should have a vote and not a veto in the evolving nature of Jewish life. In other words, the law itself is contextual and therefore changeable. This contrasts with the *Or HaChaim* text, which claims that questioning is acceptable but changing the law never is. While for some this concept is a heretical denial of the omniscience and omnipotence of God and the eternal covenant, for others the ideas of Kaplan are liberating, rational, and organic to the true nature of change. The Reconstructionist movement of Judaism, stemming from Kaplanian ideas, doesn't treat *halakhic* alterations in a wanton fashion, but it does accept changes and abrogation that are considered reasonable for today's society.

I would add that even referring to Judaism as an evolving religious civilization reduces the Jewish identity and experience to more of a religion and less of a culture, philosophy, and way of life. This idea is echoed in a 1901 essay by Bernhard Felsenthal:

> "Judaism" and "Jewish religion" are not synonymous terms. "Judaism" is more comprehensive than "Jewish religion." For "Jewish religion" is only a part of "Judaism." Judaism is the composite of collected thoughts, sentiments and efforts of the Jewish people. In other

---

[19] See Mordecai M. Kaplan, *Judaism as a Civilization: Toward a Reconstruction of American-Jewish Life* (Philadelphia, PA: Jewish Publication Society, 1981).

words, Judaism is the sum total of all the manifesta-
tions of the distinctively Jewish national spirit.[20]

Rabbi Israel Friedlaender, a prominent figure in the early Conservative movement, wrote in 1919:

> It was a fatal mistake of the period of emancipation,
> a mistake which is the real source of all subsequent
> disasters in modern Jewish life, that, in order to fa-
> cilitate the fight for political equality, Judaism was put
> forward not as a culture, as the full expression of the
> inner life of the Jewish people, but as a creed, as the
> summary of a few abstract articles of faith, similar in
> character to the religion of the surrounding nations.[21]

Jewish emancipation of the eighteenth to twentieth century was,
on one hand, a positive movement toward a long-awaited acceptance
of Jews as full citizens of Europe, and, on the other hand, a forced
Protestantization of Jewish thought, culture, life, and practice. It
abridged, defined, and colonized Jewish life to fit a Christian model.

The Quickening
"There is nothing new under the sun" (Eccl. 1:9). "Heresy" and
"holy" have always lived hand in hand, and that which is deemed
one or the other may actually be its opposite. The quickening of the
world's pace creates an opportunity for all communities and opinions
to face one another. The facing can be relational and well-intended
or oppositional to the point of violence. It can also be indifferent
or dismissive, which often creates ignorance and misunderstanding.
My sister, brother, and I are examples of the quickening of Jewish
life all facing each other with (fortunately) acceptance and love. An
Orthodox-gone-Reform rabbi's children living in a Kaplanian world

---

[20] Emma Felsenthal, *Bernhard Felsenthal, Teacher in Israel* (New York: Oxford University Press, 1924), 212.

[21] Israel Friedlaender, quoted in Andrea Most, *Theatrical Liberalism: Jews and Popular Entertainment in America* (New York: NYU Press, 2013), 5.

of an evolving civilization coming to terms with itself concurrently. One of the children is Ultra-Orthodox and upholds a steeped, rich observant life. Another lives out his Jewish identity mostly through the lens of anthropology. Anthropologist Marshal Sahlins, himself a secular Jew, theorizes that culture is merely a learned and shared system of symbols. My brother values the symbols and experiences of them without a *halakhic* allegiance. Defining myself seems to be a more difficult task, which is perhaps informative of the labeling process in general. Perhaps it's an easier task to label others than it is to define ourselves. I am a gay ordained Reform rabbi. While a proud graduate of the Hebrew Union College–Jewish Institute of Religion, I consider myself to be trans-Jewish—meaning I learn from people across the spectrum and from as much of Jewish life as is attainable.

The use of the term trans-Jewish is intentional. I am proud of the transdenominational work of the Academy for Jewish Religion California and fervently believe in its humane, dialogical, and educational mission. At the same time, I resist the utilization of the word denomination due to its correlation to the Christian backdrop of its origin, as well as its reduction of the totality of Jewish life into a "religion" or "faith" construct. Cultures, philosophies, and people do not ultimately benefit from being compacted and belittled into smaller categories in order to make them more palatable to the dominant culture. One of the results of this reduction is that we ourselves experience decreasing levels of self-understanding.

The Reckoning

Proclaiming that Judaism is an evolving process and people is its reclamation. There are also devolutions that are a natural part of survival. Codifications and simplifications of complex thinking into Jewish law to make it more understandable to the common person; minimizing a people's vast history and civilization to make it more palatable for a dominant culture; and grasping to gain a sense of who we are to ourselves—all these are aspects of the survival and evolutionary process. Perhaps in our reckoning of all that comprises who we are is a messianic understanding (supernatural or simply the result of our conscious endeavors), that well-intended and thoughtful heresies and heretics, both within and outside of Judaism, can lead to a sacred survival where the apostates and righteous are, in a sense, one and the same. Or, at the very least, when the host asks the real heretic to please stand up, everyone rises together in recognition of mutual understanding and acceptance. We are not impermeable and this is a core value of Jewish education. We are reliant on one another and responsible to model rich relationships built on the foundation of multiple ideas and pluralistic interdependence.

Part 3:

Journeys

Polyphonic Judaisms
Jonathan L. Friedmann

My life as a "professional Jew" began in my senior year of high school when I co-founded a klezmer-fusion band called the Rabbinical School Dropouts. The name was not a jab at rabbinical school as such, although we were decidedly secular. It started as a corny twist on the song "Beauty School Dropout" from *Grease*. But, as we developed our unique brand of "esoteric space klezmer," we began to see the name as a philosophical position. In our abstract, outsider's impression of what rabbinical school entailed, the institution was a metaphor for the purist fossilization we heard in preservationist klezmer groups. Our original tunes—which we measured as 25% klezmer, 15% jazz, 11.5% rock, 10.5% classical, 10% Middle Eastern, 9% Indian, 7% free improvisation, 5% Afro-Latin, 2% East Asian, 2% Spanish, 2% circus, and 1% Native American—were miles away from a *Fiddler on the Roof* aesthetic. The far-flung sounds were welded together through an array of instruments: clarinet, bass clarinet, saxophones (soprano, tenor, alto, baritone), oboe, English horn, bassoon, trombone, cello, bass, mandolin, electric guitar, autoharp, melodica, piano, toy piano, keyboards, drum kit, tabla, congas, theremin, and more.

Rabbinical School Dropouts was the sole Southern California group among the mostly East Coast ensembles signed to Tzadik Records' Radical Jewish Culture (RJC), spearheaded by avant-garde jazzer and McArthur Fellow John Zorn. The series got its name from the 1992 Munich Art Projekt music festival, which Zorn curated under the title "Radical New Jewish Culture." Subsequent shows and festivals in New York's Lower East Side initiated a loosely organized movement (or "moment"[1]) of musicians who unimpededly fused Old World klezmer with any sound that would stick to it. Through free and seamless hybridity—defined by RJC scholar Jeff Janeczko as "the mixing of various forms, styles, and elements within what is generally considered 'Jewish music' with other non-specifically Jewish musi-

---

[1] Tamar Barzel, *New York Noise: Radical Jewish Music and the Downtown Scene* (Bloomington, IN: Indiana University Press, 2015).

cal genres"[2]—musicians examined and reexamined their borderless, multi-layered, and highly idiosyncratic Jewish identities.

For those involved in RJC, cultural blending is a natural and authentic mode of being Jewish: "tradition," whatever that term means, requires the reformulating, reimagining, and relevantizing of inherited traits, musical and otherwise. Stressing this point, Zorn's RJC mission statement opens with a quote from Gershom Scholem:

> There is a life of tradition that does not merely consist of conservative preservation, the constant continuation of the spiritual and cultural possessions of a community. There is such a thing as a treasure hunt within tradition, which creates a living relationship to tradition and to which much of what is best in current Jewish consciousness is indebted, even where it was—and is—expressed outside the framework of orthodoxy.[3]

From its cloudy beginnings in late medieval and early modern Europe, klezmer—a term originally used for musical instruments (from *klei zemer*, "vessels of melody"), later applied to musicians (*klezmorim*), and assigned to a genre category only in the twentieth century—was a mixture of musical styles that came in and out of fashion at weddings, markets, fairs, circuses, restaurants, parades, theaters, and other festive venues. At Jewish and non-Jewish events, *klezmorim* had to be versed in peasant dances, salon dances, light classical works, military marches, devotional melodies, and other musical vocabularies. As they traveled from venue to venue, traversed geographical, social, and cultural landscapes, and played with non-Jewish musicians (especially Roma), the sundry flavors gradually merged into a fluid and organic

---

[2] Jeff Janeczko, "Negotiating Boundaries: Musical Hybridity in Tzadik's Radical Jewish Culture Series," in *The Song is Not the Same: Jews and American Popular Music*, ed. Josh Kun (West Lafayette, IN: Purdue University Press, 2011), 138.

[3] John Zorn, "Radical Jewish Culture," www.tzadik.com. Quote from Gershom Scholem, "Israel and the Diaspora," reproduced in David Biale, *Gershom Scholem: Kabbalah and Counter-History*, 2nd ed. (Cambridge, MA: Harvard University Press, 1982), 8.

whole. In this sense, contemporary groups are not so much "radical" as they are keeping the ever-expanding musical melting pot boiling.

As a living and constantly adapting mode of expression, virtually all music is hybrid to some extent. The history of the Jews is filled with dispersed and migratory sub-groups who have incorporated local sounds from the places they settled. Folklorist and singer Ruth Rubin put it this way: "Jewish folk music is as diverse and variegated as the Jews themselves."[4] What distinguishes "postmodern" mixtures from older blends we intuitively recognize as klezmer is the degree and overtness with which ingredients are stewed together. In our age of music streaming, mass migrations, cross-cultural collaborations, and boundary blurring, openminded musicians inevitably experiment with more styles.

After about a decade, my band died of natural causes. We were no longer in our late teens or early twenties, and a confluence of pushes and pulls intervened: graduate school, new jobs, new spouses, new locations, new children. My focus shifted from practitioner to scholar, and from string instruments (cello, guitar, mandolin, bass) to singing. The themes of pluralism and hybridity followed me into a master's program in religious studies, where my coursework focused on sociology, anthropology, religious syncretism, and new religious movements. I also began studying voice and cantorial repertoire with my late mentor, cantor-composer William Sharlin, whose own life was filled with tensions between preservation and innovation, Orthodox upbringing and Reform vocation, *bimah* and Broadway, camp songs and musical modernism, emotionalism and rationalism, tribalism and universalism. These educational encounters resonated with my non-conformist, self-styled Jewish identity, which found comfort in complexity, tension, ambiguity, the irrelevance of labels, and the insufficiency of definitions.

My life revolves around three indefinables: music, religion, and Judaism. Neither the particulars nor the generics of music are universally agreed upon. Musical sounds exist in a variety of "dialects," and no single conception of what constitutes music is applicable cross-

---

[4] Ruth Rubin, *A Treasury of Jewish Folksong* (New York: Schocken, 1950), 11.

culturally. A definition that satisfies Western principles often fails when applied to a non-Western society. Arriving at a suitable definition of music is further complicated by the fact that ideas about sounds change over time. Composer Edgard Varèse famously called music "organized sound."[5] However, such organization is not only heard in the conventional building blocks of music—rhythm, meter, pitches, durations, dynamics, etc.—but also in ostensibly non-musical sounds, such as raindrops, spoken words, construction machinery, and car alarms. The past century has stretched the musical envelope to include a seemingly endless platter of possibilities. A growing inclination to treat non-human animal sounds as musical (zoomusicology) expands the question of what constitutes music beyond the realm of humans. The *Encyclopedia Britannica* states, "while there are no sounds that can be described as inherently unmusical, musicians in each culture have tended to restrict the range of sounds they will admit."[6] Philosopher Lewis Rowell avoids the "dangerous task" of defining music, recommending an inclusive approach instead: "let *music* signify anything that is normally called *music*."[7] Combining the above, we are left with a crude approximation of a working definition: Music consists of tightly or loosely organized sounds that adhere to strict or lenient parameters of a given culture or sub-culture, and are accepted by a consensus large enough to qualify it as "normally called music." Yet, a catch-all definition, however broad, is hopelessly problematic, as hearing something as music always depends on a web of culturally and personally determined factors, which are themselves subject to shift depending on the feelings or agendas of a group or individual.

The same is true of religion. Attempts to define something as historically, culturally, and structurally varied as religious systems invariably fixate on certain aspects and exclude others. Many scholars who have waded through the mud of competing definitions have resigned to "embrace the mystery," to use a religious aphorism—or at least concede that it's more productive to study each manifestation

---

[5] Edgard Varèse, *The Liberation of Sound* (New York: Orion, 1966).

[6] *The New Encyclopedia Britannica*, vol. 8 (2003), 422.

[7] Lewis Rowell, *Thinking About Music: An Introduction to the Philosophy of Music* (Amherst, MA: University of Massachusetts Press, 1983), 1.

on its own terms. Max Weber declined to posit a definition in the opening sentence of his influential treatise, *The Sociology of Religion* (1920): "To define 'religion,' to say what it is, is not possible at the start of a presentation such as this. Definition can be attempted, if at all, only at the conclusion of the study."[8] Tellingly, Weber's book does not conclude with such a definition. Closer to our time, scholars have broadened the scope of religion to include holistic therapies, fitness regimens, sports and pop culture fandom, "civil religions," the churches of Elvis, John Coltrane, and Beethoven, and other occupiers of grey areas and border zones. Like music, there is no single definition of religion that addresses all phenomena that might be called religion. Whether the proposed delineation is substantive (what it is), functional (what it does), or polythetic (what it shares with others), there will always be outliers and hard cases.

Despite its status as a "major world religion"—a distinction owing more to its influence than size—Judaism is hard to squeeze into the religion box. Religion is a modern Western category; in many cultures, past and present, comparable concepts or equivalent terms simply do not exist. Daniel Boyarin has argued that native Jewish languages have no parallel word for what we now call "Judaism."[9] Instead, the idea of Judaism as a compartmentalized set of practices and beliefs has its origins in eighteenth- and nineteenth-century Germany, where the Jews' (imperfect) integration into the nation-state required a restructuring of an all-encompassing lifeway into a Protestant-imitative model, wherein religion (or "faith") is a private matter set apart from one's civic allegiance. Efforts to abstract Jewishness from the fabric of life clashed with centuries of Jewish experience. There was no template for being a (wo)man of the street and a Jew at home. Attempts by emergent Jewish denominations to extract the "essence" of Judaism, articulate its core principles, and establish boundaries between competing movements only highlighted the unease with which a once

---

[8] Max Weber, *The Sociology of Religion*, trans. Efraim Fischoff (Boston, MA: Beacon Press, 1993), 1.

[9] Daniel Boyarin, *Judaism: The Genealogy of a Modern Notion* (New Brunswick, NJ: Rutgers University Press, 2018). See also Leora Batnitzky, *How Judaism Became a Religion: An Introduction to Modern Jewish Thought* (Princeton, NJ: Princeton University Press, 2011).

organic system became an artificial construct.

Today, we are left asking whether Judaism is a religion, ethnicity, race, culture, nationality, all of the above, none of the above, or some combination of the above—a question transcended in some sense by the inclusive, if nebulous, notion of "Jewish peoplehood" (*Amiut Yehudit*). Endeavors to isolate a conviction or set of convictions all professing Jews share—aside, perhaps, from self-identification as a Jew—ultimately come up short. Ambiguity is woven into the patterns of Jewish history, as Jonathan Z. Smith observed: "We need to map the variety of Judaisms, each of which appears as a shifting cluster of characteristics which vary over time."[10] By pluralizing Judaism and acknowledging that its constituent elements morph and consolidate and morph again over time, Smith reminds us that "map is not territory" (another of his favorite phrases): the concepts, categories, and classifications we use to describe a thing are not the thing itself.[11]

The reality of history is always messier than the historiographer can record. Innumerable actors, divergent experiences, opposing attitudes, variant customs, and other intricacies are necessarily cleaned up or glossed over by the researcher, whose work is carried out with a limited (and sometimes agenda-driven) set of interpretive tools. What we tidily call "normative" or "mainstream" Judaism is a scaffolding of many contextually derived layers that defy either/or distinctions: the Tanakh with Midrash; the Vilna Gaon with the Baal Shem Tov; Kabbalah with Haskalah; religious personalities with cultural contributors; sacred with secular.

In a 1982 essay on the pluralistic nature of Jewish ethics, Rabbi Harold Schulweis cautioned against reducing Judaism's "multi-dimensional character" into a container of "apodictic certainty and finality."[12] His introductory remarks are as fresh today as when they were written:

---

[10] Jonathan Z. Smith, "Fences and Neighbors: Some Contours of Early Judaism," in *Imagining Religion: From Babylon to Jonestown* (Chicago, IL: University of Chicago Press, 1982), 18.

[11] Jonathan Z. Smith, *Map is Not Territory: Studies in the History of Religions* (Chicago, IL: University of Chicago Press, 1993).

[12] Harold M. Schulweis, *The Single Mirror of Jewish Images: The Pluralistic Character of Jewish Ethics* (Los Angeles, CA: University of Judaism, 1982), 1.

To be open to the evolutionary character of the tradition presents an obstacle to those who would settle for doctrinaire denominational definitions. Judaism is an old-new religious civilization reflecting the ideologies, beliefs and practices of a world people whose career extends across many continents and centuries. It mirrors a variety of responses to challenges of different environments...Jewish theologies and philosophies respond to the different moods of a people lonely in the desert, joyous in the vineyards, frightened in the valley, exultant on the plains. Portions of Judaism are consequentially this-worldly and otherworldly, ascetic and materialistic, ethnocentric and universalistic.[13]

If we must continue to use old, flawed terms to describe the phenomenon known as Judaism (and we probably must), then the best we can do is put them in the plural: Judaisms, traditions, ethnicities, civilizations, cultures, traditions, and maybe even religions.

During the second year of my master's program, I enrolled in cantorial school at the Academy for Jewish Religion California. The seminary's transdenominational approach was appealing. Like Abraham Joshua Heschel (though I wouldn't dare put myself in his league), I was "not a noun [Jew] in search of an adjective."[14] Exposure to the different streams and tributaries of Jewish thought and practice—both Sephardic and Ashkenazic—harmonized with my eclectic disposition. Still, the name of the school rubbed me the wrong way. In addition to perpetuating a historically clumsy contortion, placing "Jewish" and "Religion" side by side implicitly delimits what constitutes the Jewish. Even as an ordained cantor, with all the responsibilities pertaining thereto, I consider myself a practicing secular Jew: my identity blurs distinctions between sacred and mundane, cultural and devotional, study and service, ethnic and ethics. For me, holidays and life-cycle

---

[13] Ibid., 1-2.

[14] John C. Merkle, *The Genesis of Faith: The Depth Theology of Abraham Joshua Heschel* (New York: Macmillan, 1985), 12.

events are as much cultural expressions as they are spiritual experiences, and the accompanying music, in particular, evokes numerous, simultaneous, and equally valuable responses: emotional, conceptual, nostalgic, spiritual, associational, epiphanal.

I soon realized that the Academy's name was just a name. The program's inclusiveness went beyond denominational voices to address the reality that, for many Jews, the need for community, connection, and continuity (however defined) rank much higher than denominational allegiances or even ritual observances. The training prepared me to serve and educate Jews (and non-Jews) from all points on the observance spectrum. Over the past decade and a half, I have served in Reform, Conservative, Reconstructionist, and Humanistic congregations—the latter resonating closest with my personal philosophy, though I remain a committed non-movementarian.

Unlike most seminarians, I did not hope to someday land a fulltime pulpit. My aspirations were largely academic: combining my scholarly interests in religious theory, Jewish studies, and the music of the Jews. My first four musicology books were published during my AJRCA student days, along with a bundle of journal articles. During my final year of cantorial school, I entered a Ph.D. program in Hebrew Bible. There, too, pluralism proved to be the only reasonable lens through which to view the subject. Research for my dissertation, examining the various roles of music in biblical life, revealed the philosophical and theological variety of Tehillim (Book of Psalms)—a centuries-spanning compilation popularly viewed as the "prayer book" of the Second Jerusalem Temple. Among the many examples of "intra-Psalmic theological pluralism" are God's relation to the dead (Ps. 6:5 vs. Ps. 139:8–10), whether or not God sleeps (Ps. 44:24 vs. Ps. 121:4), alternative creation accounts (e.g., Pss. 8:1–8; 33:6; 74:13–14; 104:24–26), and different ideas about God's location (e.g., Ps. 115:3 vs. Ps. 139:8–10)—just to name a few.[15] Applying the old adage "Two Jews, three opinions" to Tehillim, we have 150 psalms, 225 opinions.

---

[15] See Jaco Gericke, "Philosophical Perspectives on Religious Diversity as Emergent Property in the Redaction/Composition of the Psalter," in *The Shape and Shaping of the Book of Psalms: The Current State of Scholarship*, ed. Nancy L. deClaissé-Walford (Atlanta, GA: Society of Biblical Literature, 2014), 41-52.

Similar diversity is found almost everywhere we turn: biblical genres, rabbinic literature, medieval thought, modern commentaries, and all strands of biblical criticism.

I have been on the faculty of AJRCA since fall 2010, the semester after my graduation/ordination. My position as professor of Jewish music history and, more recently, as associate dean of the Master of Jewish Studies Program, has allowed me to oversee more than two dozen theses, guide students through an assortment of independent studies, and develop and teach a plethora of courses: Jewish music history, Jewish musicology, musical diversity, music in the Hebrew Bible, history of the cantorate, Jewish environmental ethics, *piyyutim* (liturgical poems), and 21st-century Judaism. Each of these topics is a complex mosaic that resists dogmatic viewpoints and black-and-white explanations. While some of the textual, philosophical, and musical formulations derive from denominational settings, others do not. When heard or read together, the impression is akin to a Havdalah candle, with various braids forming a whole of distinguishable parts. Forcing these subjects into a single denominational perspective—where ideas, histories, and aesthetics are filtered through a preconceived framework—would require a type and level of sanitizing and apologetic maneuvering that the subjects do not abide. Their natural habitat, like mine, is unresolved polyphony: tension without need of release.

Of course, the goal of Jewish professional education is to train future leaders. As interesting as the course materials may be, the end is not *Torah lishma* or study for its own sake. By swimming in an abundance of examples, ideas, theories, methods, trends, innovations, interpretations, evolutions, and retrenchments, my students (ideally) develop a degree of dexterity and flexibility that will help them serve, teach, and lead communities that are, increasingly, as amorphous, fragmented, multifarious, and beautifully messy as the concepts of music, religion, and Judaism themselves.

A Living Nation
Judith Aronson

When the faculty of the Academy for Jewish Religion California began talking about what we meant by calling ourselves "transdenominational" or "nondenominational," and furthermore writing about it, I was eager to begin. Yet, all I could think about was the journey I have taken in my long life as a Jew, and as a Jewish educator. I began sifting through the file boxes that live in more than one place in my home and stopped when I found a small book called *Blessings and Songs* that was awarded to me by Agudas Achim Sunday School in Hartford, Connecticut for good scholarship in 1943. It started me thinking about the stops along the way and my connections with synagogue life.

My very first memory was of being in the men's section in my grandfather Izzy's arms when I was about four years old. My uncle Irving was in the boys' choir and I felt very safe. It was many years before I found out that Izzy was a founder of that *shul*. In 1902, the congregation awarded him an 18k gold medal which reads, "Presented by the First Zurower YMBS [Young Men's Benevolent Society]." I have looked the organization up at YIVO and know that my grandfather was their founder and longtime president, and had already purchased a cemetery property for them. They had a place where they could *daven* (pray) together. Obviously, I am proud of the roots and where they have led me. In 1946, when my grandparents attended my bat mitzvah, he said, "I have never seen anything like this in my life, but I like it." To this day, I recognize how fortunate I was to have him in my life. He worked in the garment industry but loved the outdoors. In his retirement he finally had a yard where he could garden and produce organic fruits.

We moved to Connecticut just before my brother's bar mitzvah and were pleased to find an Orthodox shul within walking distance. That synagogue, Agudas Achim, has now moved from the historic building I attended. When I looked at this history online, I discovered that the founders were Romanian Jews who described themselves as from

"Sepharad." I think of my connection with them every Pesach when I open *The Complete Passover Cookbook* by Frances R. AvRutick, their *rebbetzin*. She was a lifelong friend of my mother's and I rely on her tzimmes recipe, among others.

Although I loved their Sunday school, we also lived almost next door to a Conservative synagogue called The Emanuel Synagogue. I belonged to a Brownie troop there and had friends in the school. By the fifth grade, I persuaded my parents to spend the $100 to become members, although that was a lot of money for them. But The Emanuel became the center of our lives and we all attended services weekly. My brother eventually became an elected leader and also was trained as an assistant cantor.

The Emanuel had a distinguished faculty. My sixth-grade teacher in my first year there made it clear that our subject was theology. Among my other teachers were people who would influence me for life. They included the principal of my secular high school, who was also my ninth-grade teacher and who gave me my first teaching job at the age of sixteen. It was a second-grade class in a school maintained by the National Council of Jewish Women, which reached out to families who could not afford synagogue membership. I discovered that I had a talent for storytelling when, on Purim, my students ran to the open windows and called to the people walking up the street, "Haman is dead." Storytelling has stood me in good stead for the rest of my life.

Although I felt strongly connected to Conservative Judaism, by the time I was in my twenties, I felt there was a disconnect between theory and practice. I was asked to join the sisterhood leadership and wondered whether I belonged in that social milieu. Two moments stand out in my memory from that time. First of all, I was invited to someone's home on the eighth day of Pesach and was served *chametz* (food with leavening). I took these things seriously and felt disappointed. I also participated in a Friday night service and carefully prepared the Hebrew I was asked to read. One member shocked me by saying that it seemed as if I knew what the Hebrew meant. Why would anyone read publicly without studying the text and search for the meaning?

In that same period of time, I began to teach at the oldest Reform congregation in Boston, which had its own journey from Orthodox founding to membership in the Union of American Hebrew Congregations (now Union of Reform Judaism). What they never gave up was a daily *minyan* (quorum), which I began to attend when I needed to say the Mourner's *Kaddish*. The service was thoughtful and I felt at home with it. The senior rabbi saw me looking for texts in their library and asked if he could help. I told him that I did not feel I was prepared to teach Jewish history with only one college level course under my belt. He kindly told me that he would prefer an enthusiastic beginner to a jaded professional and offered to help me with a reading list. My respect for Reform Judaism was growing.

When my family needed to join a congregation, we decided that Temple Sinai of Brookline was worth the try. What I sensed was an authenticity. It was the beginning of my journey as a professional Jewish educator. A few years later, I was asked to become director of education at another Reform congregation with a knowledgeable rabbi. He had grown up in Brooklyn and actually studied with a distinguished Hasidic rebbe. He mentored me for several years and finally told me that I was ready to become part of the National Association of Temple Educators (NATE). Because of his encouragement, I joined and took my first trip to Israel.

By the time I was in my thirties, I had belonged to and worked in all the major denominations. Each one gave me comfort and security in its time. Concurrently, I became an active member of several national organizations and began to attend conferences sponsored by NATE and the Coalition for Alternatives in Jewish Education (CAJE). Scholars of Torah and Judaism expanded my scope of Jewish text study. In my mid-forties, I recognized that I felt the need for serious study and enrolled in a master's degree program in Hebrew Scripture and history of religion at the Harvard Divinity School. Not only did I learn the grammar of Biblical Hebrew, but I met people of every world religion and recognized basic similarities and differences in their literature and practice.

In 1980, I moved to Los Angeles to become director of education in a very large Reform congregation. By chance, its rabbi also came from Boston and went to yeshiva with Rabbi Harold Schulweis, a Conservative rabbi and a great teacher. We had similar ideas about practice, and the services had, for me, an acceptable amount of Hebrew. That summer, my father died and at the end of *shloshim* (thirty-day mourning period), I attended a national conference at the University of California, Santa Barbara. I arrived on *erev* Shabbat as part of the organizing committee. I got up early the next morning to attend a *minyan*. Services were in a three-story classroom building. The top floor housed the Reform *minyan*, the middle floor had the Conservative *minyan*, and on the main floor was the Orthodox *minyan*, led by a young *rosh yeshiva* (head of school) from the Midwest. Ten people had not gathered on either of the top two floors, and so I made my way to the Orthodox service. I ended up as the only person who stayed for the *davening*. They pulled a sofa up beside where I was seated, and that was their *mechitza* (partition separating men and women). The other women would not accept a *mechitza*. I knew I wanted to say *Kaddish* for my father and happily sat by myself in this makeshift women's section.

For the rest of the conference, the *rosh yeshiva* would find me in the dining room where we had our meals, and introduced me to all the Orthodox educators who arrived that Sunday for the week. He would explain that although I was not used to a *mechitza*, I was happy to respect the tradition because it was more important to me to *daven* and say *Kaddish* than it was for me to uphold a Reform point of view.

This incident started me thinking about who I was as a Jew. Some years later, my daughter's best friend who came from a Unitarian background became engaged to a British Moroccan Muslim. They asked me to conduct their wedding ceremony. I told them that I was not a clergy person, but the bride said I promised her I would do this when she was twelve years old. Although I did not remember this, I was fond of her and got a certification to conduct weddings. Word spread and for a time I did a variety of ceremonies, including one at the Harvard Faculty Club in Cambridge, Massachusetts, and almost all of them were intermarriages of one sort or another. When a Jewish couple asked me to perform their wedding, I sent them to see the bride's rabbi. Whatever happened, she returned and begged me to officiate. I recognized that I allowed myself to do something unusual because that was, and always would be, my iconoclastic nature.

When I think about my own family today, I am excited by the great diversity of practice in the next generations. One of my great-nephews invited me to perform his wedding at 10,000 feet above sea level in Colorado. His wife was not Jewish, but they told me they would raise Jewish children and today are following through with their daughter, the sixth generation since our family arrived in the United States. Another nephew, a brilliant chemical engineer with a Ph.D., has become Orthodox, spending the last two years in Israel studying Talmud. When he is done with his studies, he will have an arranged marriage, something that hasn't happened in the family since our ancestors were in Europe, six generations ago. It amazes me that through the history of my average Jewish family, I understand why I am proud to be writing about nondenominationalism.

When I reached retirement age, I was asked to substitute for a year teaching the basic course in Jewish Education at the University of Judaism in Los Angeles (UJ; now American Jewish University). For thirty years, I was a member of the clinical faculty of Hebrew Union College's School of Education, meaning that I studied monthly with my colleagues at HUC and mentored about thirty of their graduate students who also taught in my religious school. I had never taught a graduate course, per se, but the UJ had a well-developed curriculum and I felt close enough to the Conservative world to do justice to their carefully scripted course design. I worked hard until I felt confident.

About the time I was grading my UJ students, I received a phone call from the president of a new school called the Academy for Jewish Religion California, who had been told that I could develop an education course for the school. It was a great challenge, but I was intrigued that it is was not sponsored by any of the denominations. Meeting the diverse faculty of distinguished scholars, I felt honored to know them and have a chance to teach with them.

As I am writing about the direction my life has taken, it suddenly occurs to me that there was an important course I took at Brandeis University during my junior year. Much of the content of that course was collected by Nahum N. Glatzer twenty years later in *Modern Jewish Thought: A Source Reader*. It is a book I have returned to over the years. I assign one chapter at the beginning of my graduate level Judaic courses. It is written by Simon Rawidowicz, who also taught at Brandeis in the 1950s. Sadly, I never studied with him then, but knew of his brilliance. The chapter is called, "Israel: The Ever-Dying People." His supposition is that every generation of Jews feels like it might be the last. In my lifetime, meeting young Holocaust survivors made me wonder how they lived when their families and friends all perished. One of them, a handsome young man who had been on a death march, graduated with me from high school, married immediately, and had several children. Then, at the age of twenty-seven, he died suddenly of a heart attack. The sorrow of his loss stays with me to this day. But, when I read Rawidowicz's take on what it means to be Jewish, I am comforted by his closing paragraphs:

> If it has been decreed for Israel that it go on being a dying nation, let it be a nation that is constantly dying, which is to say: incessantly living and creating—one nation from Dan to Beersheba, from the sunny heights of Judea to the shadowy valleys of Europe and America.

> To prepare the ground for this great oneness, for a Jewish realism built on it, is a task which requires the effort of Jewish scholarship and statesmanship alike. One nation, one in beginning and end, one in survival and extinction! May it be survival rather than extinction, a beginning rather than an ignominious end—one Israel, *yisrael ehad*.[1]

There is no room in my life to doubt that whatever way Judaism is practiced, we are surely more alike than we might think and all committed to the Jewish generations to come.

---

[1] Simon Rawidowicz, "Israel: The Ever-Dying People," in *Modern Jewish Thought: A Source Reader*, ed. Nahum N. Glatzer (New York: Schocken, 1977), 142.

A Journey to Spiritual Wholeness
Eva Robbins

I am a rabbi, a cantor, and a Jewish artist. I serve one master, *HaShem* (The Name), which I have internalized as *YudHayVavHay*, four letters that essentially speak of unity, oneness, and relationship with all Jews. As one of G-d's emissaries and an ambassador for our spiritual path, I try to speak for a Judaism that embraces all; that is egalitarian, open, accepting, and like the Tree of Life itself, rooted in a past yet spreading its branches in all directions. While on my own Jewish journey these past many decades, I often feel puzzled by its direction since my starting point was a Conservadox Judaism, newly formed by hundreds of Holocaust survivors in my hometown of Toronto—most particularly, my own parents, who were determined to re-create a close facsimile of their Eastern European Jewish life, once alive and thriving. Yet being a Jew, whether religious or cultural, was a marker for hate, antisemitism, and ultimately annihilation. Their suffering and loss needed a familiarity and comfort zone in the midst of change and new surroundings. Their belief was in hope and a future, bringing three children into the world. But the Judaism we received was limited, narrow, not visionary, and far from accepting.

As a young woman I experienced a tradition that needed to perpetuate male dominance, male voices, and male leadership. Though seating in the sanctuary was mixed, with male and females next to each other, the *bimah* (pulpit) was limited to male lay-leaders and male staff, and the *hazzan's* voice, which directed the congregations' prayers to G-d, had to be male, supported by an all-male choir. Though I had to attend *cheder*, Monday through Thursday religious school following secular school, a mere block away, as the only girl in the class my desk was set in the back of the classroom and I was given a very clear message: "your voice is not to be heard." This was a hard pill to swallow as my spirit was not only attracted to the sounds of our *tefillot* (prayers), but, to understand a tradition that went back thousands of years, somehow seduced by the mystery and untold stories that held me captive.

On the High Holy Days, I watched men and women, who held a trauma that was unspeakable, sit in community dressed as if going to a concert, but engaged in ongoing conversation, ignoring our rabbi's sermon—an act of total disrespect. It was a reflection of how unengaging or uncompelling his words really were, or perhaps an indication that this Judaism couldn't inspire its flock, especially a younger generation in search of connection. I heard words that reflected fear, especially concerns about assimilation, intermarriage, and protection. And I saw pain and a flood of tears as the *Yizkor* (Memorial) service began and I was rushed out, too young to share in their loss.

As I moved beyond this newly formed "*shtetl*" as a teen to other parts of Toronto, where the nouveau riche settled, I learned there were other kinds of synagogues, one in particular whose architecture reminded many of a Western European gothic church and with the name Holy Blossom. It was a Reform congregation, but for my traditional family and their cronies, it was an unacceptable form of Judaism, likened to a church, particularly since it had an instrument, an organ, that accompanied the cantor. This was considered blasphemy by many Orthodox and Eastern European Conservative Jews, who maintained continued mourning for the destruction of the Holy Temple in Jerusalem. The most recent trauma of the Holocaust easily merged with this embedded grief that many Reform Jews were willing to shed. I became more and more sensitive to the markers that created boundaries and critiques of the other, seemingly to split a community based on doctrine, appearance, and practice. I was bewildered, but in typical personality formation, there was a subtle and unvocalized influence seeping inside my soul. My own narrow-minded views settled deep in my unconsciousness only to surface years later.

Uninspired, and basically rejected because of my sex, I emotionally detached from Judaism. Denied the right of passage to become a bat mitzvah, my tradition had set me apart and at arm's length. I understood that marriage and family were my purview, and being the "good girl," the role most second-generation females embraced, I was a wife by age nineteen, relegated to creating a Jewish home—special foods for Shabbat and holidays, lighting Shabbat candles, going to synagogue on Rosh Hashanah and Yom Kippur, and attending family gatherings for the two most important Jewish holidays in North America, Passover and Hanukkah. Without any real knowledge of Jewish history, ideology, or purpose of the Jewish calendar, I felt a void. I was reminded to keep kosher, honor my parents, and show up when necessary. My *neshama* (soul) resonated to *nusach* (modal prayer chant) and the songs of my people. But this was religion and dogma that, for me, lacked soul and spirit.

After five years in an abusive marriage, stranded in Cincinnati thousands of miles from my family, it was time to move on. Divorced, working as a secretary, and beginning evening classes at the University of Cincinnati, I knew I needed more. After a transformative experience at the Gestalt Institute, I sought other places where I could build self-confidence, grow, and perhaps even re-connect with my Jewish roots. Hebrew Union College had a branch just up the street and I heard that one of their students was the acting rabbi at Hillel, a truly transdenominational institution. Intrigued, I found myself with an appointment to meet this rabbi who not only ran Gestalt groups, but led "creative" services, a term I had never heard growing up.

One week later, I walked into a small old house that smelt of musty antique books and met Rabbi Steve Robbins. I was introduced to a wholly and, dare I say, *holy* different Judaism. With my deeply seated prejudices, I learned it was okay to ask questions, to sit in a room with a guitar and sing contemporary music, and walk off the pages of tradition to reshape *tefillot* and hold religious dialogue that felt relevant and meaningful. It was okay to understand the past, be in the present, and let both shape the future. Though it is not the focus of this essay, my own future was reshaped as well, as this unlikely Reform rabbi not only answered many of my questions, but also stole my heart. We were married a year later in the little Hillel house where we met.

Discovering a different Judaism was quite exhilarating, though the "*haimish*" and deeply embedded tradition I grew up with still held a place for me. But I was on a new circuitous path of weaving the old and the new into a tapestry where the boundaries were permeable and the *shitach* (partnership) felt energizing. Steve's seven years of Hillel work opened me to the challenge of serving Jews from all denominations. I sat with Orthodox, Conservative, Reform, and nondenominational young Jewish adults wanting to express their own comfort levels of religious expression, with multiple services often going on at the same time, and yet they would sit at tables, together, on Shabbat, eating, talking and singing, breaking the barriers of their past and present to be in camaraderie, sharing joy and laughter. They joined in prayer on the High Holy Days led by a Sephardic young man, as well as myself chanting *Kol Nidre*, a woman expressing the traditional text, which a cantor in the community, David Unterman (*z"l*) was willing to teach me. A Reform cantor, Unterman was so unlike the Eastern European teachers who endearingly called me "Chavalah" but could never permit themselves to hear my voice in song. In 1972, I witnessed the first woman ordained as a rabbi when I attended Steve's ordination at Hebrew Union College in Cincinnati. In 1974, in Berkeley, California, two men (rabbi and cantor) and a woman (myself) stood together leading a thousand Jews of all denominations in some of the most moving and deeply held prayers in our tradition. This was an unforgettable experience that began to sow the seeds of what would become the future of Judaism.

Along with satisfying work and a wonderful community, we expanded our family when our first child came into the world. Birthing Rachael was one of the most incredible Jewish and human experiences I've ever had. I felt truly connected to the Divine and understood the power of creation. The experience moved me to begin using my hands to create through techniques of quilting, applique, and embroidery. I was inspired to make a Jewish quilt as a first Father's Day gift, which led to my first commission from Sharon and Michael Strassfeld and the beginnings of a new line of work. This new form of expression guided me on a journey of discovery of both old and contemporary Jewish objects. It ultimately led me to create a post-Holocaust *mezuzah* (decorative case for a doorpost), which reflected my growing pluralistic Judaism. Based on a Victorian sewing technique known as "crazy quilt," I took remnants of all of my projects and commissions and pieced them together. For me, each represented a fragment of the Jewish community, stitched and embroidered together into one piece with the *mezuzah* scroll at its center. This fabric ceremonial object came to represent all that was developing inside of me: the different colors and textures were unified and held together by the one essential belief in Judaism, the *Shema*—that G-d is one and we are all one with G-d. I knew in my heart that both art and music could transcend boundaries and unify those of different ideologies or denominational backgrounds.

While in Berkeley I met two of the greatest forces who changed the face of Judaism: Rabbis Shlomo Carlebach (z"l) and Zalman Schachter-Shalomi (z"l). In the mid-1970s, these men shared new melodies, ancient stories and teachings, and the hidden spirituality of Kabbalah, Hasidism, and Mussar. Slowly and intently, these "Orthodox" rabbis were speaking to young Jews totally disenfranchised by a more rational and dogmatic Judaism. The Holocaust, assimilation, identity, and intermarriage had been a forced focus in sermons throughout the continent and in articles and books for mass consumption. But as the 1970s and 80s reflected a new generation of Jews, a deeper conversation was emerging, though the word "G-d" had barely been expressed. The Divine presence seemed far and remote, and I had heard stories of young and middle-aged adults traveling to far-off India in search of a more spiritual religion—one where practice was both accessible and emotional, and where the body and the mind could connect. Meditation was falsely understood as only part of the Eastern religions. It was in our own holy texts all along, particularly in the visions of the prophets that gave rise to Jewish mysticism. By the turn of the first century, just before the destruction of the second Holy Temple (70 CE), *Merkavah* Judaism (based on Ezekiel's vision of the chariot with fantastical creatures and magical movement) took flight (author's pun). Our teachers and rabbis had rejected these writings, either fearing the impact of such material on us common folk or because they were, themselves, unschooled in the mystical and Kabbalistic literature, following in the footsteps of their seminary teachers.

Both Shlomo and Zalman abandoned their orthodoxy. They not only became voices for innovative teaching, but were willing to bring it to both men and women, crossing a clear line drawn by many traditionalists. Being well aware of the soulless experience of Judaism that many espoused, they brought the forgotten teachings of great inspirational Kabbalists and Hasidim, reframed traditional texts, and offered spiritual practice that would open the minds and souls of so many. An inner-directed experience of Jewish life was being offered—what these Jewish leaders described as renewing the connection between Jews and their practice and identity. The language of prayer took on new meaning, often removing any male-centered references, and couching it in a way that resembled the inner struggles and conflicts of contemporary Jews. Commentary and textual analysis reflected modern concerns, so that one could relate to ancient material and finally have a stake in its validity.

Others followed suit: maverick rabbis willing to teach outside the box and outside the conventional path, with newly formed *chaverot* (communal shareholders) and *minyanim* (small groups that studied and prayed together), some within the borders of synagogue life and some totally independent, often rejecting conventional and denominational institutions.

It was in the midst of this revolution that I discovered a path to the cantorate. My husband left his conventional rabbinic post at a large Beverly Hills synagogue, and together we, along with many expats of that congregation, decided to form a new synagogue, where this form of spiritual emphasis, family education, and deep textual study became central. Without a budget for a cantor, I volunteered to lead services and occasionally prepare bar/bat mitzvah students. I had just graduated from UCLA as an interior designer, anticipating a new career where my burgeoning business as a Jewish artist could be expanded. But as I became more and more entrenched in Jewish work, I realized I had found a way to express my true, deepest passion, squelched decades ago by my Conservadox teachers. I could now sing the music of my forefathers and foremothers, melodies that had taken residence in my consciousness, despite my continued rejection. *"Mi-Sinai"* tunes (sounds so deeply heartfelt it was as if they were created at Mount Sinai along with the tablets), traditional modes of prayers, and life-cycle melodies being written at summer camps by Jewish American folk singers all joined in a circle of friendship, old and new, traditional and innovative, and my toolbox became deeper and wider for musical expression.

By the time I was 50 I had mentored with all the cantors in Los Angeles that would have me (Cantors Nate Lam, Joe Gole, Jeremy Lipton, and Sam Radwine). Men from different denominations opened their hearts and their shelves to this eager woman who wanted to lead others with dignity and integrity. I realized the icing on the cake would be to finally take ownership of Torah and become a bat mitzvah. Thirty-seven years after my thirteenth birthday, I too would join the ranks of all of those boys and girls, as well as male and female late-bloomers, to stand before witnesses to chant my *parshah* (portion) and teach its meaning. Somehow the many years of travelling through Conservative, Reform, and now Renewal territory had formed a Judaism that felt personal, spiritual, relevant, and unifying. It was beyond the bounds of any one denomination, and yet it felt like an integration of the best of each. I could now share with my students and congregants an authentic voice that connected me to my ancestors and from where I came, could be experienced in the present, and hopefully inspire the future.

In the year 2000, my husband Steve informed me of a conversation he had with Rabbi Stan Levy. They both felt the need for a new seminary on the West Coast. Individuals had been asking them for private mentoring and personal ordination, but both Steve and I felt that this was inappropriate and pretty *chutzpadik* (audacious). Fortuitously, Steve and Stan were approached by the Academy for Jewish Religion (AJR) in Yonkers, New York to explore the possibility of a sister school on the West Coast, one that had the hallmarks of being "transdenominational"—a word Steve had shared with me. Though my experience led to an inner knowing of this word, I had never heard it before. I knew it felt right. I also knew, at that moment, that being a wandering cantorial student, going from mentor to mentor, what was needed was a cantorial school on the West Coast. I insisted that he and Stan pursue this possibility if a seminary was going to be created. I had studied with many wonderful cantors and knew a faculty would be very easy to put together.

And so it was. A sister school to AJR would be birthed. The Academy for Jewish Religion California (AJRCA) in Los Angeles would ordain both rabbis and cantors, and I applied to be one of its first ten students. Despite the many years of mentoring and working, I knew that sitting in a classroom with other like-minded Jewish men and women could broaden my base of knowledge, not to mention expose me to the many teachers we would attract from every denomination. Within a few years, the two AJRs parted ways, and AJRCA shaped its own identity.

The students all shared one commonality: we were late-bloomers, changing careers or discovering, later in life, our true passion. As the Academy developed, younger students joined, and the program expanded to include a chaplaincy and master of Jewish studies programs. In all the years of its existence, the one thing that holds AJRCA together is a strong respect for each other's experiences, Jewish points of view, and affiliations.

Like Hillel, students come from an array of Jewish walks of life, so creating communal experiences can be challenging. Praying together tests the openness and boundaries one is willing to cross. In my own work as a cantor, I have walked a fine line between traditional musical modes, modern melodies, and moments of inner work that requires silence. It is a transdenominational journey, a fusion of the finest of each, interwoven into an experience of the eternal *now*, holding the past, being fully in the present, and influencing the future. For a number of years, I became part of the administration as director of admissions and recruitment and was often the first face prospective students would meet. My journey and deep understanding of AJRCA's birth made it possible to engage others in this unique model of Jewish expression, discovering many hidden travelers in the Jewish community. As a teacher in the rabbinic program, I had an opportunity to expose my deeply beloved prayer modes to rabbinic and chaplaincy students along with modern melodies. I wanted them to feel comfortable with traditional sounds and respect their place in Jewish practice, and hopefully connect to them in a soulful way. So, it is not about denomination, but the breadth of Jewish expression, grounded in the past, along with those from the present, and holding both with honor for the future. It is a partnership in a mixed marriage where songs and melodies, English or Hebrew, can share the same space and complement each another.

When I officiate at a life-cycle event, people ask what denomination I belong to. I tell them, "let's talk after I finish." Often confused—for they hear "Conservative" sounds (traditional melodies in Hebrew), Reform sounds (songs in English), Renewal sounds (commentary that includes Hasidic, Kabbalistic, and spiritual content)—I explain that this is transdenominational Judaism. I don't represent one denomination only, though I am affiliated with the Cantors Assembly, the professional cantorial organization of the Conservative movement, where I originally found a home. The Conservative cantors reminded me of my youth and listening to the great Hazzan Louis Danto of my congregation, Beth Emeth Bais Y'huda, who was also a close friend of my family. Somewhere in the recesses of my soul, I still feel at home with the early sounds of my past and the generation of people who spoke Yiddish, pinched my cheeks, and patted me on the head. I know they meant well, though I often felt discounted and invisible because I was female. But I also know that I am fortunate to have found my place, to be able to sing for so many that left this world before their time, and to be part of a rebirthing of Judaism that soars beyond boundaries and dogma.

In 2010, when it became clear that my cantorial work would be limited, since my partnership with my rabbi-husband had to find new rhythms due to the medical challenges he lived with, I decided to pursue the rabbinate. I inquired at the Conservative seminary in Los Angeles, University of Judaism, now American Jewish University (AJU). I wanted to push my limits and see if I could wrap my brain around intense text study. Applying to the AJU, I was told, meant I would have to test out of all the classes I had taken at AJRCA, since the Academy had not yet received its accreditation, which was finally granted in 2013. That was more than I had bargained for, so I went back to AJRCA to take a class and test the waters of my comfort level. I received a warm welcome from my teachers and appreciated that this program would better fit my ideological and spiritual journey.

I was ordained as a rabbi at AJRCA in 2015, and so my work has expanded beyond the musical. Rabbinic ordination has afforded me the opportunity to teach in a way that reflects the many paths of Judaism I have embraced. The transdenominational focus is less about a particular dogma and more about what unifies all denominations and all Jews. It is the spiritual focus as opposed to the religious. It is about making Torah and *YudHayVavHay* the center of Jewish life. I believe it is the core of every denomination.

In a world where people have real life struggles with loss, change, aging, loneliness, suffering, depression, relationships, fear, insecurity, and even happiness, there needs to be a "holy" center, a core to hold on to, an ability to walk one's path and find meaning and purpose. We need to see the psycho-spiritual meaning in Jewish ceremonial life and holiday celebrations. Despite the denominational focus for many, with its ideological teachings, individuals are seeking a connection to something *greater* than themselves as well as a oneness with their souls, which is deep *within* themselves.

Spiritual practices—mindfulness, meditation, Mussar, Jewish yoga, etc.—can be shared with others, even when they identify with different denominations. One of the greatest experiences I have had is in a cohort with other rabbis and cantors, all from different denominations and Jewish practices, sharing spiritual time in meditation, prayer, yoga, study, and song through the Institute for Jewish Spirituality. Teaching these practices to all Jews is a way to break through the barrier of denominations, and yet share what is humanly the same. The journey from birth to death is often experienced from one stage to another, dealing with similar concerns, worries, fears, losses, as well as joys. These human experiences, which we can share and support, are the essence of transdenominational Judaism for me. They are beyond the limitations of group membership, allowing and surrendering to what all of us share in common as Jews.

As I wrote in the beginning of this essay, I serve *HaShem*. The four-letter name is for me what ties and unifies all Jews. However, I know there are Jews who don't believe in G-d, at least in the language I speak. For some, I present it as a concept of an unknown force that helps to explain nature, creation, and the constancy of this world. Whatever the description, I have seen a response that brings some solace and/or understanding. Speaking about character, values, and ethics is for me transdenominational. When I quote *Pirkei Avot*, "Who is wise? The one who learns from every person" (4:1), it affirms for me that going beyond denominations is opening to all Jews their truth, and what they have to teach. Transdenominational Judaism allows digging into some of the most ancient texts and teachings that apply to all Jews. It means focusing on what unifies us as human beings and what supports our journeys to become more accepting of ourselves, more connected to our souls, and find what unifies Jews as a community and a people.

When G-d created a covenant with the people at Mt. Sinai, S/ He didn't ask which denomination they would like to be a part of. In the sacrificial cult, our ancestors were divided into three groups— *Kohanim* (the Priests), *Levi'im* (those who sang and served in the Temple), and *Yisraelim* (all the rest of the people). The Temple and its sacrificial cult no longer exist, so we are all one—the House of Israel. It is our deeds that really speak to who we are. Personal growth is encouraged in all denominations, whether Reform, Conservative, Orthodox, Reconstructionist, Renewal, Humanistic, or beyond. The calendar, with its rhythms and central themes, helps us focus on a richer emotional and spiritual life, and examine our behaviors, our values, and our responses.

Studying Torah, as the voice of *HaShem*, is also a means for improving our lives and staying connected to the Divine. A transdenominational approach sees the underlying human message or the mystical/spiritual understanding, neither of which falls into a denominationally limited view. For example, when G-d punishes Moses for striking the rock twice after giving instructions to the contrary—that is, to speak to the rock—we not only study how our sages understood this behavior, but also take note of the context in which it happens: literally right after Miriam, Moses' sister, has died. We try to identify with this man who, according to the text in Torah, was immediately bombarded by complaints from the people after the well of water disappears with Miriam's death. It is clear he has not been able to grieve the loss of his beloved sister. This is an opportunity to see ourselves as Moses and look at how we might respond in a stressful moment or to pressure from others. We use the text as a way to open up our inner life, gain a better understanding of what triggers our own emotional responses, bring a deeper understanding of ourselves, and perhaps open a conversation about how we can mitigate against rash behavior or misdirected anger. We can explore together what possible tools are available to us so that we can gain more equanimity in our lives. This kind of intra-personal approach to studying Torah goes beyond denominational ideology. Finding meaning in ancient texts not only connects us to our heritage and the journey of our ancestors, but can also be a tool to improve our own lives. For some it can also create a pathway to the Divine and G-d's lessons for every Jew. When the past and the personal intersect, it brings life to both the ancient text and the one who studies it.

The focus of certain *mitzvot* and laws, certain customs, and pathways of prayer and study are expressed in denominational ways. They can create a place of safety and community, sharing familiar thoughts and feelings about how to live a Jewish life. But for some leaders in the Jewish community, what is most important is finding the common ground where we can meet and relate to one another, crossing boundaries, and connecting on a human level, sharing our similarities at our very core. Seeing the Divine spark in each individual, and not the box of denominational identity, makes it possible to relate to one another, honor one another, and respect one another. My personal journey has led me to go beyond a denomination to a place of spiritual wholeness, to *sheleimut*, where I hope I can guide others to embrace a wider view of being Jewish and creating peace, *shalom*, amongst our people.

Part 4:
Teaching

Reflections on Teaching Liturgy in a Nondenominational Context
Tamar Frankiel

During the thirteen years I taught Introduction to Liturgy (Tefillah) in its various incarnations at the Academy for Jewish Religion California (AJRCA), I was often asked by my colleagues from other institutions, "But how do you manage prayer?" The question implied: "We understand you can teach Tanakh, Talmud, and history in a nondenominational setting. We understand that you can teach *halakha* (Jewish law), even while knowing not every student is committed to it. But prayer—everyone has to do that together; you must choose a prayer book. By the very nature of communal prayer, you must be requiring some people to pray in ways different from their personal choice and from the synagogues they will serve. Prayer in American synagogues is, after all, essentially denominational."

That last statement seems indisputable. A community's choice when it buys fifty or a hundred or five hundred *siddurim* (prayer books) makes a clear statement: this is how we pray; this is the stream of tradition with which we identify. So that must be the case at a seminary as well.

Our premise at AJRCA was that each student could become accomplished enough in leading prayer to serve any type of devotional community. A student might not be hired long-term by certain communities, but the reason should not be his or her lack of competence in prayer. Rather, for example, it might be gender or commitment to *halakha* or their stance on social issues or certain denominational principles. While there were also different levels of such competence expected in our various programs—cantors had to master musical traditions, rabbis had to master text and the teaching of it, and chaplains focused on praying with people in less formal settings—all should be able to step up to any situation that called for leading a basic prayer service.

Now, it turns out that with this approach, it was easy to choose a prayer book for learning. It had to be an Orthodox one that had all the regularly used prayers, as well as prayers for special occasions. When the Academy opened, the standard in American Orthodoxy had become the Artscroll *siddur*. When Rabbi Jonathan Sacks produced his new translation with the Koren publishing company, we changed to that version. Under the leadership of the president and dean of the Rabbinical School, Rabbi Mel Gottlieb, our standard weekday service was established using these *siddurim*, tailored to fit the time frame of our schedule. We also acquired for the *minyan* (quorum) the recent *Mishkan T'filah* of the Reform movement and, about a decade later, the new Conservative *siddur Lev Shalem*, as alternates. (Of course, we had many more in our library for research.) As students developed their competencies, they were permitted to choose a different *siddur* or even develop a creative service when it came their turn to lead a *minyan*. We developed "*tefillah* teams," led by more advanced students with others serving as apprentices, so to speak, to lead *minyanim* on campus on a rotating schedule. Students were encouraged to introduce elements from their own prior learning or experience, so we also had contributions from Reconstructionist prayer translations and from the Renewal movement.

One of the surprises for me was how quickly the students lapsed (or advanced, depending on your perspective) into what I would call a "hidden orthodoxy." They repeatedly asked, "Which of these are we required to say?" "Exactly how do you bow?" "If we have a time limit, what can we leave out?" "Can anyone lead *Kaddish*?" and so on. Making distinctions and applying an orderly structure is a basic Jewish instinct—actually it's a universal one, but with a particular *ta'am* (flavor). Jews want to know how to "do it right," even if they will then argue for a freer, more autonomous actual practice. This has implications, as I will develop further on, for helping students understand the deep structures of liturgy.

That was our practical approach as it evolved over the years I was actively teaching. It accommodated most of the different texts and styles of prayer on a regular basis as a praying community. Let me turn to the issues in the classroom.

Prayer, Text, Structure

When I began teaching at AJRCA, I inherited the course entitled "History and Structure of the Siddur," essentially a broad survey. I discovered that most students thought they knew the structure of Jewish prayer based on their experience of Shabbat prayers in synagogues. But what that meant is they knew a few key pieces of structure: The congregation always said *Shema* congregationally—many thought "the *Shema*" was one line only—and then a silent prayer. Before and after, there were songs that differed according to one's synagogue, following the direction of the cantor or rabbi. Then the Torah was taken out of the Ark for public reading.

In other words, prayer was structured as an affirmation of faith, a time for prayer to God, and a Torah reading on certain days. Most knew there was choreography that involved bowing, sitting, and standing, though few knew it well enough to teach it. Students from traditional backgrounds—Orthodox or Conservative—were more proficient in larger versions of the structure. They knew, for example, that the *Barchu* was the official call to prayer; that a minyan was needed for *Kaddish* and *Kedushah*. But only a few had a deeper understanding, and those were students who had taken prayer seriously on a personal level or had a strong prayer leader in their home synagogue.

So my first principle in "teaching liturgy nondenominationally" was to ask everyone to take a much bigger perspective—to understand this body of prayer that we had inherited as a gift from our ancestors, shaped and transmitted over two and a half millennia. Indeed, the very approach we were advocating in our pluralistic age was mirrored in the multiple eras of Jewish devotion expressed in prayer historically. In teaching "history and structure," I was teaching students to listen to those many voices.

These voices were not, I explained, merely a cacophony. But the sequential order of prayers in the weekday service (the focus of most of my teaching) did not present prayers with their origins, nor did they conveniently offer themselves in a historical order of development. Still, one could discover in many cases the layers that had been added over centuries. The *Shema* was biblical. But the choice of these particular words for a public recitation indicated a process of selection, from dozens of passages from the Torah that could have inspired dedication to God. Indeed, our passage had been selected out of several in *Devarim* (Deuteronomy) itself that began "Hear, Israel!"

Then, at some point this recital was embedded in poetic compositions that we now identify as (long) *brachot* (blessings). The first known reference to those was in the Mishnah, which states that such *brachot* were recited earlier, in the times of the Second Temple, by the priests when they said *Shema*.

This opened up two major topics essential for understanding the voices in our prayers: *brachot*, which had biblical roots, but what *we* say reflects a different formula than most biblical blessings; and priestly practice, also with possible biblical roots, but we know almost nothing of what priests *said*. Indeed, one theory is that sacrifices were offered in total silence. (Was this a matter of "no evidence" being read as "evidence of nothing"?—a common historical problem that students needed to recognize.) We have some probable Levite songs; we have prayers attributed to kings. How did this thick book in front of us emerge from these? And again, what is essential or at least very important, and what is incidental, sectarian, or optional?

Besides recognizing strata of many voices, including the evidence of editorial voices and compilers as well as "original" sources, students had to learn how to read more carefully. Most general education, even at the bachelor's degree level, encourages students to learn by reading the textbook. This is a habit that college teachers try to break, but when in doubt, it is the students' default approach. In their major subject or in a master's program, they will have learned a little about "primary sources" or "data-based research," but with new subject matter, they will default to textbooks. And they will transfer that habit to "primary" reading as well, unless taught otherwise. So, most students tended to read the *siddur* like the morning newspaper. Except that here, instead of "facts" or "information," one would find "beliefs." The *siddur*, they thought, expressed "Jewish beliefs."

What beliefs? One God, mainly. Is that all? What other beliefs? Umm....Creation, Revelation, Redemption.

That, of course, they had found as a comfortable capsule formulation widespread in supplementary readings—behind which was

Rosenzweig, and behind him a tradition of commentators. Asked what those words meant, they recited equally formulaic explanations, and found themselves struggling to stay afloat in deep water with the concept of redemption.

I firmly insisted to students that they had to read the prayers themselves with closer attention, and equally firmly refused to assign a textbook. Under pressure, I produced a bibliography of widely read guides and commentaries by traditional and modern authors, such as the *My People's Prayer Book* series, or Reuven Hammer's classic *Entering Jewish Prayer.*[1] But I explained that those tended to give authorial glosses on prayers, and did not substitute for their own close reading.

The benefit of "Read the text!" was that small discrepancies began to show up. As one of my extraordinary teachers, Jonathan Z. Smith, loved to say, "Incongruity gives rise to thought." I suspect that is ultimately derived from "Why is this night different from other nights?" When things don't match up, when any intelligent reader can see that the text doesn't say what you *expected* it to say, a question arises. Also, when you are *told* that a prayer is about one thing, but the language does not match, a question arises.

An example is the claim that *Emet v'yatziv*, the blessing after the *Shema*, is about redemption. But it first goes on for quite a while about truth and loyalty, so what are the voices actually saying? Similarly, we often read that the first blessing before the *Shema* was composed to "refute Persian dualism," because it says God "creates all" instead of following Isaiah, where God said "I make peace and create evil." But the Isaiah passage already refuted dualism. The inquiry opens in a different direction.

As we moved toward a more sophisticated level of discussion, students learned to see literary patterns as well as textual glitches. Con-

---

[1] Lawrence Hoffman, ed. *My People's Prayer Book,* a multi-volume set on each section of Jewish prayer—weekday, Shabbat and holidays; published by Jewish Lights beginning in 1997; Reuven Hammer, *Entering Jewish Prayer: A Guide to Personal Devotion and the Worship Service* (New York: Schocken, 1994). I have also recommended two books from the Renewal movement, which help with discussions of *kavanah*: Zalman Schachter-Shalomi, *Davening: A Guide to Meaningful Jewish Prayer* (with Lawrence Kushner et al.; Woodstock, VT: Jewish Lights, 2012), and Marcia Falk, *The Book of Blessings* (Boston, MA: Beacon, 1999; re-published in 2017).

gruences in pattern between the first and last blessings surrounding the *Shema* are invisible on the literalist, newspaper-about-beliefs reading. But like the rabbit/dog drawing, once you see the pattern, you can't *not* see it, and from that day forward one can feel the congruence of the voices of angels and the voices of the Israelites crossing the sea, every time one prays.

This kind of learning cashed out in a big way when we studied the *Shemoneh Esreh*. In this portion of the course, I required every student to make a detailed chart of all nineteen blessings, as they appeared in Hebrew and English in each of four denominational *siddurim*, Orthodox, Conservative, Reform, and Reconstructionist. They had to identify specific differences in translation as well as wholesale changes in the text. Suddenly, the standard summations they had heard about the "effects of the Enlightenment on Judaism" lit up like beacons. "Now we understand what the Reformers were doing!"

They were equally surprised that Conservative prayers were virtually identical to the Orthodox, although the translations might differ—sometimes inconsequentially but sometimes with new overtones. Most did not realize how closely the Reconstructionist prayers hewed to the Conservative, except on certain key issues. And, just so they wouldn't think I was privileging the Orthodox version as somehow pure, I also brought in examples of Orthodox versions of prayers that rendered, sometimes wrenchingly, rather than translating the original Hebrew: for example, portions of the Artscroll *bentscher* for "Grace After Meals." Of course, the problem is not simply a new rendering; we are always doing that. The problem is the extent to which the changes are hidden—completely for the non-Hebrew reader, and veiled even for many who can read Hebrew, just by the realities of repeated common usage and the fact that alternates are rarely mentioned, let alone taught and discussed.

We mentioned above the topic of *brachot*. This itself could be a whole course—and one of our superb teachers at the Academy did occasionally offer it. "Blessing God"—whatever that means, certainly worth at least one class period of discussion—is arguably a frame for rabbinic Judaism itself. Rooted in God's message to Abraham—"you will be a blessing"—and the *midrashic* (interpretive) traditions about

Abraham teaching all people to thank God, it's an essential piece of any nondenominational approach to liturgy. Again, once students are alerted, they find *brachot* everywhere. Besides students discovering their wondrous variety of content, they also explored the liturgical functions of blessing, thus opening new realms for theological discussion and creative liturgy.

Meanwhile, dipping into the prayer section entitled "morning blessings" in a traditional *siddur* can be enlightening. The blessings for beginning the day are often elaborated in modern synagogue services to fifteen minutes or more, instead of being said at home privately as in ancient times. That in itself reveals a great deal about modern and ancient voices. Students are startled to realize that a considerable body of additional voluntary devotions are in *Birkhot HaShachar* (Morning Blessings). Why is there another *Shema* here? Why is the portion on incense read by some people? And the *Akeida* (Binding of Isaac)? Recitals of remembrances, of Maimonides' thirteen principles of faith....an entire history course could be written. But this, for better or worse, is largely consigned to the inessential. These were from other "denominations" whose voices are largely silent now.

The significance of *Pesukei d'Zimra* (Verses of Praise) received short shrift in the introductory course, again due to time constraints. The Academy encouraged students to take more advanced courses in Psalms and *piyyutim* (liturgical poems) to enrich their understanding of poetic literature in the framework of liturgy. What I found most helpful to elucidate, in our brief considerations, is the way the literary structure of this section aims to rejuvenate the Temple, and King David as "sweet singer," for the participants in the prayers. Of course, *tehillim* (psalms) were from ancient times a source of inspiration and comfort; but here they become a gathering place, if you will, for an imaginal congregation—contemplating the Temple, going up in pilgrimage, adding voice after voice to a vast and ultimately cosmic song. Rarely is this section used as such a contemplative technique in our services today; but our students occasionally took this inspiration and incorporated it into their creative services in our *minyan*.

The introductory course is only the beginning. With each new study of parts of the liturgical cycle—High Holidays, Festival liturgies, and other memorial days—more layers of history, more voices of prayer, can be uncovered and made accessible to the student.

Philosophical Reflections

The challenge of this work was identified in the title of a book by Mike Comins, *Making Prayer Real.* Implied for most practitioners—whether beginners or advanced among us—is making God real. But I realized, over these years of teaching, writing, and practicing, that the "reality"—of prayer, or of God—is not about belief in the usual sense. Prayer does not come to ask or answer the question "Does God exist?" and far less to engage in argument: "Can you prove it?" and "How can there be a God in a world of evil?" Nor is it meaningful to ask "Are your prayers answered?" "What should you ask God for?"

Others have suggested that prayer is measured by its effect on us. Maybe we change, instead of changing the world by getting prayer "answered." Prayer perhaps opens up the question, "What is *our* existence?" Where are we in the cosmos? What do our voices, the organs of prayer, mean in this vast universe? An ancient prayer, now half-hidden in *Birkhot HaShachar*, tries to address this question in an attitude of abject humility, similar to our High Holiday prayers: We are nothing, You are everything; all we can do is supplicate You.

This is getting closer, but not quite. The mood of that prayer may sometimes strike our hearts when we feel our vulnerability. But most days, if we show up for prayer at all, we are showing up as confident, post-Enlightenment human beings. In ways incomprehensible to people of ancient times, we have learned through industrial and technological revolutions, to exercise all manner of control. Our humility is not that we are nothing, but that we know we have not yet touched the fullness of the mystery—who we *truly* are—as a self, individually; as a people, Jewishly; and as a species, humanly.

The rabbis have said that each level of created being has its own gift. Stones have weight and dimension. Plants have growth—*tzemach*, sproutingness. Animals have movement. Humans have speech.

Prayer is the process of learning to speak the mystery into/with the cosmos. Cosmos is related to the Greek *kosmein*, lining up two sides or faces. Where they "fit," we see, feel, experience something.[2] So it is with one who prays. We line up, we "face" God, and discover whether and where we fit with God *panim el panim*—face to face. When the words of prayer resonate, there is a meeting between the two; in that moment and possibly in those words, or possibly in an image or sounds, is a theophany, a form through which we can experience the divine.

"The entire cosmos is permeated by liturgies of creation and hymns of praise," writes Thomas Cheetham, a poet and scholar of Sufi traditions. "The whole of reality is meant to be one vast Prayer. Far from being a plea sent toward a distant God, prayer is the means by which Creator and Creature are irrevocably entwined, one with the other, in mutual sympathy."[3] Moreover, prayer as liturgy is also communal, it turns to the faces of the "others" who are singing, have sung and will sing, each in his/her/their individuality.

So when we pray the Jewish liturgy, we are entering a realm where God appears through David of whom we sing; through the Temple of which we sing; through the angels at their moment of creation, of which we sing; through Moses on the plains of Moab of whom we sing; the Israelites at the sea, of whom we sing. And God appears through the Land and the City and the priests and the prophets and the sages and the ancestors and the congregation, of whom we sing. And God appears each time we chant a *brachah*, in the form of the food or the person or the event. *Aleinu*, it is on us to develop the sight and hearing and depth of feeling to live that experience fully.

---

[2] Ivan Illich, "The Scopic Past and the Ethics of the Gaze," quoted by Thomas Cheetham, *After Prophecy: Imagination, Incarnation, and the Unity of the Prophetic Tradition* (New Orleans, LA: Spring Journal, 2007), 88.

[3] Cheetham, *After Prophecy*, 18. Quoting Henri Corbin: "Prayer is not a request for something; it is the expression of a mode of being, a means of existing and of causing to exist, that is, a means of causing the God who reveals himself to appear, of 'seeing' Him...in the *form* which precisely He reveals in that prayer act." Cited from *Alone with the Alone: Creative Imagination in the Thought of Ibn 'Arabi*. The approach of Corbin, particularly as interpreted by Cheetham for modern English speakers, is highly thought-provoking, as it lives on the fine edge where philosophy, vision, poetry, prayer, and the arts come together. However, it is beyond most students unless they have actual training in philosophy or critical thinking about the arts. So, I don't teach this in my classes. I do try to introduce the key concept of the "imaginal" that is not imaginary.

In modern times this way of experiencing prayer, and of seeing the world as a refractor of divine light, has almost completely died away. It seems astounding that generations could have thrown away a book full of poetry—our *siddur*—as though it were fake news from yesterday's newspaper. But we did—we lost the poetic, the imaginal sensibility, the depth dimension of reality that makes life worth living. Fortunately, we did not lose the music; but we too often try to fly with just that one wing. Still, it is possible to recover this mode of experiencing through the imaginal, to once again sing/pray the world into being; and that is what can restore our life.

Denominational, Nondenominational, Transdenominational, Post-denominational or Pluralistic: Does the Nature of the Institution Really Matter When Teaching Certain Courses?

Joel Gereboff

Establishing rabbinic seminaries for the purposes of training and ordaining rabbis to serve all Jews in America has been a recurrent practice in American Jewish history. The founders of the two earliest successfully launched rabbinic seminaries, Isaac Leeser of Maimonides College (founded 1868, closed 1873) and Isaac Mayer Wise of Hebrew Union College (1875–), sought to serve all members of the growing American Jewish community. To be sure, each of these towering figures held particular positions regarding how Judaism (as each understood it) ought to respond to the challenges of modernity, with Leeser leaning more toward retaining traditional elements and Wise envisioning changes over time. The publication of the Pittsburgh Platform in 1885 made blatant the alignment of Hebrew Union College (HUC) with the growing Reform movement and propelled another group of leaders to launch the Jewish Theological Seminary in 1886 to preserve the knowledge and practice of what they saw as historical Judaism. But the Jewish Theological Seminary (JTS) from its beginnings, and long into the twentieth century, while serving as an alternative to HUC, sought to avoid classifying itself as being either Orthodox or Conservative. In this regard it also aimed to, and did, train rabbis for diverse segments of the American Jewish community. In time, explicitly Orthodox institutions emerged, such as Rabbi Isaac Elchanan Seminary (1896) and Hebrew Theological College (1921), which sought to replicate *yeshivot* of Europe in staking out the range of such denominationally identified schools.

In 1922, Stephen S. Wise established the Jewish Institute of Religion (JIR) in an effort to meet the needs of all American Jews. Although Wise was a Reform rabbi, he saw JIR as not aligned with any denomination. The institute employed faculty, scholars and rabbis, with various personal religious identifications. When JIR was amalgamated with HUC in 1950, and with JTS at that point being clearly Conservative, there was no explicitly nondenominational seminary. But in 1956, Louis I. Newman and others continued the vision of Stephen Wise in founding what in time became the Academy for Jewish Religion in Yonkers, New York (AJR NY), to train clergy for *klal yisrael*—the entire Jewish community. AJR defines itself as a pluralist institution. Before other pluralist institutions came into existence, the Reconstructionist Rabbinical College admitted its first students in 1968. The Ziegler School of Rabbinic Studies, a Conservative school, admitted its initial group of students in 1993, who were the first rabbis to be ordained entirely in a West Coast institution. In the last years of the twentieth century and the beginning of the twenty-first, however, additional seminaries not affiliated with any denomination emerged. The Academy for Jewish Religion California (AJRCA) offered its first classes in 2000. It labels itself a transdenominational institution. In 2003, Hebrew College in Boston launched its pluralist rabbinic program. Finally, the efforts of Rabbi Zalman Schachter-Shalomi to "renew" Judaism resulted in a more formalized structure of the transdenominational ALEPH ordination program in 2002. The history of rabbinic seminaries in America raises many questions. What has accounted for the success or failure of each school? How did schools define and redefine themselves over the course of their existence? Why did many efforts to create schools to serve the needs of the entire Jewish community often fail? Have institutions not affiliated with any particular denomination, party, or movement succeeded? Answering these questions requires detailed analysis of each institution, and more generally, correlation with broader trends in American Jewish history and the nature and significance of religion in America.

Two questions, however, have intrigued me for some time. First, what practices and policies of seminaries, especially of denominationally affiliated ones, serve to communicate to students "denominational identity"? The second question—one I will address in this essay—is whether some courses are largely taught with similar learning outcomes and similar pedagogic and substantive assumptions irrespective of the denominational or nondenominational identity of the school. I will address this latter question by discussing one of the two areas of instruction for which I have been responsible for many years at AJRCA, the Introduction to the Bible sequence of two courses.[1] I will speak about the course objectives I have defined, as well as some of the pedagogic choices I have made. In particular, I will make clear how I seek to offer an academically rigorous course, while at the same time speaking to the personal and professional development of students as future Jewish clergy and Jewish leaders. I will also share some of my impressions of how various students respond to being introduced to an "academic approach" to the Bible, an approach typical for courses in Hebrew Bible offered in secular higher education settings. The primary difference between courses in these two institutional settings is that students in Jewish institutions are generally all Jewish and are pursuing training as Jewish professionals.

All of the non-Orthodox denominational seminaries,[2] as well as the pluralist seminaries,[3] have one or two required courses that introduce students to the formation and content of the Hebrew Bible and to critical methods that shape the analysis of the various elements of the Bible.[4] For example, at HUC the core curriculum taken in the second

---

[1] The other course I teach is The History of Jews and Judaism in the Second Temple and Early Rabbinic Eras. I have discussed my approach in "Teaching about Jesus and Early Christianity in US Rabbinic Schools," in Zev Garber ed., *Teaching the Historical Jesus* (New York: Routledge, 2014), 69–79. There I also review how aspects of this period of history are addressed in various rabbinic seminaries. My sense is that, for the most part, the overall course goals and content are quite similar in the various institutions. This is due in part to the commitment to academic rigor on the part of faculty at the various institutions and their efforts to communicate up-to-date scholarship on these matters.

[2] HUC, RRC, JTS, and Ziegler School of Rabbinic Studies at the American Jewish University.

[3] I will use this term to refer to AJR NY, AJRCA, Hebrew College, and ALEPH.

[4] I consulted the websites for each of the seminaries and have spoken informally with students who have attended many of them. Most of the websites contain general descriptions of their Introduction to the Bible courses. The Orthodox Seminaries, RIETS, HTC, and Yeshivat Chovevei Torah (YCT) do not include courses on the Bible in their curricula. RIETS students may take courses in the Revel Graduate School of Yeshiva University. The website asserts, "The men and women who study at Revel find themselves in a genuinely nondenominational school with extraordinary faculty in Jewish Studies. The professors at Revel have without exception published highly

and third years "consists of foundational courses that examine the language and literature of a variety of disciplines, different critical approaches to those disciplines....Students take courses in Bible [Bible I (Pentateuch) and Bible II (Prophets)], Hebrew language, etc. These courses provide students with a strong grounding in Jewish texts and traditions." JTS requires that during the first year of study students take Bible, "A two-semester survey of the Tanakh with the perspective of modern biblical scholarship and with the aim of developing a personal and professional relationship with our foundational text." As part of the American Jewish University, the Ziegler Rabbinic School asserts, "We believe in the principle of *Torah Li'Sh'ma*—Learning as an intellectual and inspirational endeavor that embraces academic scholarship and the efforts of all Jews to explore their shared heritage through the formal and informal study of Judaism and the other great civilizations of the world." As a rabbinic school adhering to Conservative Judaism, "The curriculum [of Ziegler] reflects a commitment to tradition and change. What remains is a reverence for text as the sacred harvest of our people's encounter with the divine." Courses in biblical studies "build on its progression of Humash, and then of Humash and Rashi to incorporate other scholarly and contemporary modes of reading and studying the Bible, including Biblical source criticism, literary approaches and others." The catalog details that Bible 506, Introduction to the Bible, assumes that "The Bible is a complex collection of writings composed centuries ago by people whose

respected books expanding the frontiers of Jewish learning." But the description of Revel includes the caveat, "At the same time they experience an environment suffused with a commitment to the authentic letter and spirit of historic Judaism." These dual claims may explain how Revel introduces students to the Bible. Bible 503 provides an "Introduction to major issues and movements relating to the formation, transmission, translation, and interpretation of Hebrew Scripture." But, from what I have been able to determine, the course only discusses these questions in relation to the second and third portions of the Tanakh—Neviim and Ketuvim—and does not take up questions about the formation of the Torah or the Chumash. In this way, unlike rabbinic students in non-Orthodox seminaries, RIETS students appear not to engage historical critical approaches to the Pentateuch. Several Orthodox scholars, however, have spoken of the emergence among Orthodox thinkers of a more systematic engagement with historical critical approaches. See, for example, many articles on thetorah.com as well as Marc Shapiro's essay, "Is Modern Orthodoxy Moving Toward an Acceptance of Biblical Criticism?" *Modern Judaism* 37 (2017): 165–93.

problems, interests and ways of life were often very different from our own; yet, its influence permeates many aspects of contemporary religious faith communities as well as general Western culture." As a denominationally affiliated institution, Reconstructionist Rabbinical College (RRC) has a curriculum that "is an expression of the Reconstructionist approach which is a progressive approach to Judaism. We immerse ourselves in the riches of Jewish civilization and its constant evolution." The Biblical Core of the Foundation Years' Civilizational Core Sequence, taken in the first year of study, "explores the history, literature and thought of the biblical period. Students will trace the evolution of the Bible and devote special attention to the emergence of a distinctive Israelite worldview in the context of the ancient Near East." All of the non-Orthodox denominational institutions treat the Bible as having a history to its formulation, as reflective of developments of ancient Israel set within the broader Ancient Near East. All students are introduced in these courses to a variety of critical approaches to the Bible—methods of analysis that are shared among scholars of the Bible.

The pluralist or transdenominational seminaries have very similar courses, though they vary in terms of their sequencing, the depth of study, and their broader set of learning outcomes. Hebrew College states that it "promotes excellence in Jewish learning and leadership within a pluralistic environment of open inquiry, intellectual rigor, personal engagement and spiritual creativity...We share the conviction that education is the key to Jewish vitality, and we are devoted to rigorous study of the full breadth of Jewish religion and culture." It goes on to relate to that "The Rabbinical School curriculum is a rigorous academic program. Its thematic and practical approach nourishes your mind and spirit as you prepare to serve the world as a rabbi." Hebrew College views the Chumash as the foundation of "our tradition" and students learn "to interpret it contextually as well as examining a range of commentaries from ancient Midrash...to Hasidic masters, feminist readings and contemporary literary analysis." But it goes on to note, "Never far from our learning is the question of what the text means for us today." AJR NY underscores that it is a pluralistic rabbinic institution that recognizes "the legitimacy of multiple points of views and approaches, both historically in the Jewish tradition and in the interplay of contemporary Jewish movements and schools of thought." Students at AJR NY "will demonstrate competence in Jewish texts, history and culture. This encompasses competence in traditional and academic approaches to reading and interpreting biblical, rabbinic, liturgical and philosophical texts." Students are introduced to the Bible via Bible 501, which has the following course description: "This course will introduce the student to modern critical studies of the Bible...Various methodologies used by biblical scholars will be introduced to the students. The many meanings of the text and the centrality of the Bible in the Jewish world will be emphasized throughout careful study."

ALEPH: Alliance for Jewish Renewal defines its mission as "To fully embrace a contemporary egalitarian Judaism as a profound spiritual practice and social transformer...ALEPH contributes to Jewish Renewal by supporting new creative efforts that draw upon the rich legacy of Jewish mystical/Hasidic traditions and the deep wisdom of Jewish life and practice." Its curriculum includes "both academic coursework and the full range of experiences that prepare an individual for spiritual leadership. Academic requirements are comparably rigorous as those of any respected liberal seminary." Students take Biblical History and Civilization I and II. Part I is "an intensive survey of the major movements, themes and developments in the evolution of Israelite/Jewish civilization from the birth of Israelite religion and people to the end of the biblical period....Students will become familiar with the major methodologies and disciplines of biblical studies and will encounter approaches of some of the most prominent scholars in the field." But the description goes on to note, "While the course will focus mostly on the scholarly and religious perspectives concerning biblical history, text and culture, there will also be opportunities to assess what we learn together from a spiritual perspective. We will also always consider how students can teach biblical history in ways that will make it meaningful and relevant to today's Jews." Finally, AJRCA seeks to gather "from the wisdom emphasized in the disparate denominations, including the powerful ideas found in each of those movements, but not being beholden to one particular denomination."

It sees Judaism as "not monolithic—sages from different centuries add to its profound wisdom as it adapts to new circumstances while maintaining its eternal principles and values while evolving through time." It requires a two-semester sequence, TN 3101–02, to introduce students to the study of Tanakh. "The courses will study the content and structure of biblical books with commonly used Jewish commentaries in English, and will provide an overview of critical methods, major literary theories, and important archaeological research that has bearing on biblical studies."

This review of the curricula of both denominational and nondenominational rabbinic schools demonstrates a significant overlap in terms of the content and goals of introductory courses in biblical studies. All share the conviction that the Bible, including the Chumash, has a history to its formation and that source and literary critical approaches are essential to understanding the various units of the Bible. Programs stress the academic nature of their study, while also noting that they want students to think about the wisdom and spiritual value of these texts and how they might transmit these insights to Jews to develop meaningful connections to these sources. Although the courses are not fully interchangeable, they are sufficiently alike that the common features appear to be primary, with the more specific institutional approaches also being present.

I offer several additional observations on these courses. First, I would account for their similarity in terms of the underlying assumptions these "liberal" forms of Judaism hold regarding the historical nature of Judaism. Moreover, all rabbinic schools stress that they are graduate level academic institutions. As such, they seek to be academically rigorous and offer courses that, in terms of their core contents, are similar to those of graduate programs in secular universities. Teachers of these courses see themselves as part of the broader community of biblical scholars. Second, this shared approach to Tanakh is not typical of Orthodox rabbinic schools, at least in terms of their formal curriculum. No Orthodox institutions have required courses in Tanakh. Moreover, although there has been significant discussion within some Orthodox circles of how to deal with historical-critical approaches to biblical materials, moving beyond declaring such methods and assumptions to be heretical, the formal education of rabbinic students in Orthodox seminaries does not take up these matters. As a consequence, the assertion by the nondenominational schools that they are "pluralistic" is thrown into question. While such schools do engage in many courses grounded in the views of Orthodox rabbis and scholars, and while some of these schools have faculty and students who identify themselves as Orthodox, it appears that ordinees of these non-Orthodox, pluralistic schools are not hired by Orthodox institutions. Graduates of these schools do serve *klal yisrael*, in communal institutional settings such as JCCs, retirement homes, communal day schools, and Hillels, but not in Orthodox synagogues or schools. By contrast, ordinees have taken up pulpits in the range of liberal Jewish institutions.

In my remarks until now I have underscored the academic aspects of courses in Tanakh. But even the above selective citations of the goals of these schools and their courses in Tanakh make evident that these offerings go beyond the strictly academic by seeking to engage students in biblical texts as Jews who are training to become Jewish professionals. In my concluding observations I will describe how I pursue these goals in my classes and also share student reactions to their introductory study of Tanakh.

I indicate to my students that they should think about the biblical texts we study with three questions in mind. What have you learned about the Tanakh, especially in terms of its setting in ancient Israelite times and in relationship to the Ancient Near East? This is the overtly academic learning outcome of these courses. For this part of the course students read a variety of essays and books, including *The Jewish Study Bible*, Marc Brettler's *How to Read the Bible*, Marvin Sweeney's *Prophetic Literature*, and William Dever's *The Lives of Ordinary People in Ancient Israel*. On a second level, I ask students: What is your personal, your Jewish (and human) response to the material and issues covered? What do the texts mean to you? Finally, I want students to consider how they might take what they have learned, their knowledge of Tanakh, and work with it professionally. The two latter sets of questions—personal meaning and professional use—move beyond the Bible courses I teach in my role as a professor at a secular, public university. But I do underscore to students that while in the end they need to develop their own personal relationship with the Tanakh, they should do so in an informed manner. I also stress that the overall goal of exposing them to critical biblical scholarship is to enhance their ability to parse, analyze, and understand biblical texts and to see them as reflecting and shaping the lives of those who composed, transmitted, and were exposed to them. In this way, I want students to appreciate that religious texts must be understood in terms of the human beings who stand behind them. Grasping the connections between these issues and concerns and the contexts of ancient Israel will enhance the students' abilities to engage with Jews with whom they interact and teach. It will enrich their ability to understand the concerns, wishes, hopes, and fears of such people and create a dialogue with biblical materials and the ways of life connected to those sources.

Beyond continually raising questions like these throughout the two introductory courses in Tanakh I offer—the first on Chumash and Former Prophets and the second on Latter Prophets (Neviim) and Ketuvim—I include several assignments that seek directly to have students learn about Jewish approaches to these texts and to ponder some of the personal and professional issues noted above. I seek to have students become familiar with the entirety of the Chumash by requiring them to outline the text over the course of ten weeks. Beyond ensuring they gain a basic sense of the contents and sequence of units of the Chumash, this exercise is meant to have students begin to develop their own interpretive skills. I make clear that the outline must be selective, and that each week they must create their own titles for the elements of their outlines.

In addition to seeking to increase the breadth of their knowledge, I also include a weekly assignment that has students begin to analyze particular passages in depth. I pick one chapter of the Tanakh they have outlined that week, usually one that raises provocative questions—such as the creation narrative in Genesis 1, the story of Dinah in Genesis 34, the Ten Commandments, or Moses' farewell address in Deuteronomy—and each student examines how one of the commonly used English-language commentaries analyzes this chapter. Each student chooses a commentary such as Plaut, *Etz Hayim, Women's Torah Commentary*, JPS, Stone or Hertz Chumash, or online commentaries, and writes up and shares with the class his or her analysis of that commentary's approach and substantive observations on the assigned chapter from the Tanakh. In this way, students are exposed as a group to a range of commentaries. I ask them to consider what assumptions each commentator makes about the Tanakh, and what sources of information they use to interpret the texts—classical commentators, materials from the Ancient Near East, or anthropological or feminist theories, for example. Beyond increasing their sensitivity to the features of the biblical text, the overall goal of this exercise is to enhance their analytic skills of reading secondary sources and to ensure that, collectively, students gain a sense of the range of contemporary interpretive traditions.

In the course on Neviim, using Michael Fishbane's JPS Haftarah commentary, students study the *haftarah* (Prophetic selection) that will be read in synagogues the coming Shabbat. Here, again, the goal is to enhance their textual skills, even if they are working in English—the language that most of those whom they will teach and interact with employ when reading the Bible. In addition, Fishbane often concludes his comments on each *haftarah* with remarks that speak to various post-biblical Jewish understandings of the meaning and significance of the Tanakh. His comments, along with the students' careful reading of this selection from Neviim, pushes students to think about the personal meanings and potential professional uses of these sources.

One of the most challenging aspects of teaching Tanakh in the above manner is that it requires that students think seriously about the nature of the Tanakh, its origins, and its status and authority in their lives. Students at AJRCA come from a variety of Jewish backgrounds and with varying knowledge of the Tanakh and the study of it. This is one way in which AJRCA is pluralistic. While some students have taken university-level courses in the study of the Bible, and on some level have begun to think about the character of the Bible and its historicity, meaning, and significance—and realize that it has human origins—for many students, these courses introduce notions that are often quite disturbing. Anyone who teaches Bible with a historically critical approach is very familiar with these concerns. My goal is for students to address these issues in an informed manner. The same week that I have students read and analyze Richard Friedman's *Who Wrote the Bible*, I also have them read a number of essays that expose them to some of the diverse understandings of revelation and the history of the formulation of the Bible that Jews have held over the centuries, including those espoused now. These include essays found in *The Jewish Study Bible*, a work they use throughout the course, as well as *Etz Hayim*, thetorah.com, and discussions of the various reactions to Benjamin Sommer's *Revelation and Authority: Sinai in Jewish Scripture and Tradition*. Students also read several essays that relate how various teachers of Tanakh in Jewish day schools have worked with historical critical methods and their students' reactions. Finally, for the last week of my courses on Neviim and Ketuvim, I have students read Marc Brettler's chapter in his coedited book, *The Bible and the Believer: How to Read the Bible Critically and Religiously*. My overall intention in these assignments is to foster informed and serious reflection leading to each student developing their own position on the meaning and importance of the Bible. In this way, like colleagues at other Jewish seminaries, I strive to have students think about the Bible personally and professionally, while integrating and responding to academic approaches to it.

Over the years, as already alluded to above, students at AJRCA have shared a range of reactions to the course. While a few had already engaged with biblical materials in a systematic manner and been exposed to historical critical methodologies, most either come from "traditional" Jewish educational settings, where these issues are generally not addressed, or from more liberal contexts, with very limited knowledge of the Tanakh. Nearly all students had never read significant portions from the Neviim or Ketuvim, other than the books of Ruth and Esther. Some also recognize selections from Psalms from their use in Jewish liturgy. In the end, my goal is not to compel students to adopt a particular position. But they must try to present and make the case for the views they pronounce. The conversations among the diverse students at AJRCA make for rich and thoughtful exchanges and for growth in the breadth and depth of each student's views.

All in all, based on my analysis of how the various non-Orthodox seminaries describe the general aims and orientation of their institutions, and in particular their statements about their curricular goals in Tanakh courses, I suspect that, to a large extent, introductory Bible courses in these institutions are largely interchangeable. What the schools share in common is a view that Judaism and the Bible have a history, and that Jewish texts reflect the religious strivings of Jews over the ages. All these schools also agree that the texts still have personal and spiritual value, and are essential resources for shaping the lives of Jews and for speaking to the pressing issues of today.

Whether in the future certain denominations will disappear, or whether the nondenominational schools will fail (as some have in the past), what is paramount is whether Jews will find that any of these approaches speak successfully to them and how they live their lives and find spiritual, personal, and collective purpose. Those responses will ultimately determine the fate and direction of all Jewish seminaries that seek to foster engagement with biblical texts, ideas, and ways of life.

Take Advantage of Our Emerging Culture of Collaboration
Cyd B. Weissman

Collaboration across difference is much easier and more potent than one might believe during these polarized times. One proof text I can share is the remarkable story of thirteen rabbinical schools from across geography and perspectives working together for almost three years. Participants in this inter-seminary collaboration have worked with Clal (National Jewish Center for Learning and Leadership) to offer a single course for all our students, *Leading Through Innovation*, beginning in the Spring semester of 2020. This is a first, made possible by an emerging way of doing business in the Jewish community that provides fertile ground for diverse leaders to come together for shared action. The more than 70 students who are taking this course, from London to Los Angeles, from traditional to progressive streams of Judaism, will be learning innovation tools *and* working in collaboration across theological and denominational differences.

The hope of the inter-seminary leaders is that our students will learn and apply the very practices we have employed while coming together to create this initiative. As inter-seminary participant Rabbi Jon Kelsen, dean of Yeshivat Chovevei Torah (YCT), observes: "The skill sets [of collaboration and innovation] are only going to become more necessary in the coming years, and we are all invested in generating educational experiences to best train the next generation of rabbis for the Jewish people."

A New and Fertile Way to Do Business

Three major shifts in our American society are contributing to this emerging trend in the Jewish community. The first is the economic landscape resulting from the crash of 2008. To survive drastic financial reductions, those Jewish non-profits that were able to keep their doors open post-crash have focused on identifying what they do best and do uniquely. As a result, they are narrowing their scope and right-sizing to new economic realities. Doing only what one does best opens organizations to collaborative partners who can do the rest. In the words of Peter Drucker, the legendary business consultant, "Do what you do best and outsource the rest!"[1]

In an analysis of the impact of the Great Recession, Steven Windmuller wrote in 2009 that 42% of Jewish community non-profits had joined forces with other institutions to collaborate on programs and an additional 13% had taken steps to share administrative expenses. To survive, leaders had to become willing to collaborate.[2]

Bad economics also helped leaders cultivate good virtues. Prior to the crash, I rarely saw the requisite virtues for collaboration at the communal table: those of humility, transparency and vulnerability. As an educational leader whose career has spanned four decades, I unfortunately can report too many stories of cross-organizational gatherings defined by boastfulness prior to 2008. But today, as Rabbi Cheryl Peretz, associate dean of the Ziegler School of Rabbinic Studies at American Jewish University and an active participant in the inter-seminary collaboration notes, "The world is calling on us to have a different model of leadership."

Second, the Jewish community's existential need for innovation is contributing to developing a way of working that is ripe for collaboration. Rising generations of Millennials and Gen Z-ers who are choosing not to engage, or to do so on their terms, are forcing leaders of legacy organizations and startups to admit, "We don't have all of the answers."

"Vulnerability is not a weakness," says Rabbi Elan Babchuck, head of the Glean Network, director of innovation at Clal, and a key player in the inter-seminary collaboration. "To be a spiritual innovator and to be a good collaborative partner, you have to be open to listening for the still small voice—that requires vulnerability. You have to be open to learn and to listen." Today, in order to respond to significant

---

[1] Kate Vitasek, "A New Way to Outsource," *Forbes*, June 1, 2010, https://www.forbes.com/2010/06/01/vested-outsourcing-microsoft-intel-leadership-managing-kate-vitasek.html#52532fa56736

[2] Steven Windmueller, "The Unfolding Economic Crisis: Its Devastating Implications for American Jewry," *eJewish Philanthropy*, July 20, 2009, https://ejewishphilanthropy.com/the-unfolding-economic-crisis-its-devastating-implications-for-american-jewry/

shifts in Jewish engagement and affiliation, strong leaders are growing in their ability to say, "I don't know. I need others."

Third, the rising generations are modeling a new way to work that values shared needs and interests over organizational boundaries. A number of professors and deans in our inter-seminary initiative cited the influence of their students on their own willingness to work collaboratively across our diverse organizations.

Many students are comfortable crossing traditional borders in the Jewish community. "We are a denominational seminary, but our students have different levels of identification," says Rabbi Lisa Grant, director of the rabbinical program at Hebrew Union College–Jewish Institute of Religion (HUC–JIR) in New York and a participant in the inter-seminary collaboration. "Some students will work in Reform congregations all their lives. But many will work in cross-denominational settings like Hillels or in social justice organizations." Students are teaching their teachers.

Economic hardships, a communal agenda set for innovation, and a rising generation modeling boundary crossing are key reasons for new norms and expectations in the Jewish community that foster collaboration across organizations and denominations. The work ahead for today's leaders is to take advantage of this new and fertile way of doing business. As Cheryl Peretz remarks, "The Jewish world's boundaries are diminishing, this is not a time to stand by."

Five Power Tools to Take Advantage of the Emerging Culture

To take advantage of this game-changing environment, leaders can use five power tools to foster collaboration across difference.

1. Get Out of Your Own Space

Overcoming the stubborn obstacles of our times is not a solo sport. "Things are changing. No one can do it all," says Peretz. "So you need to seek out different people with different wisdoms. When you do, you bring other people's strengths to the table."

To seek out people with different wisdoms, I attended the 2017 Collaboratory, a yearly convening of innovators in the Jewish community. I randomly struck up a conversation with leaders from Yeshivat

Maharat, the first Orthodox institution in North America to ordain women, and the ALEPH Rabbinic Program of the Jewish Renewal movement. The three of us had never crossed paths. If I had stayed at my desk responding to the demands of my inbox, we never would have come together.

After introducing myself as the teacher of social entrepreneurship and innovation at the Reconstructionist Rabbinical College (RRC), we connected around the challenge of preparing rabbinical students for our changing times. In each other, we saw possibilities and asked: Was there any opportunity to tackle this together? Who else might be interested? Those were the beginnings of our inter-seminary initiative, soon joined by invaluable others.

Kelsen, one of those valued people who joined, commented in a recent conversation about his appreciation for the chance to work with colleagues across organizations. "I've welcomed the opportunity to connect with my colleagues at other rabbinical schools with whom I share so much, yet do not have enough chances to connect."

Meeting new colleagues and potential partners is an emotional and intellectual boost. Rabbi Stu Halpern, senior advisor to the provost at Yeshiva University says, "I have been inspired by my colleagues' dedication to training aspiring religious leaders and their emphasis on having an innovative mindset in strengthening Jewish learning and living."

To find potential partners, add to your must-do list: get out of your own space. This can be done at national gatherings, which are super-sized networking opportunities; but just as helpful, and much less expensive, is sharing coffee with someone you don't know yet.

2. Identify a Shared Essential Question

The schools engaged in our inter-seminary collaboration represent important differences that enrich the multitudes within the Jewish community. Some may even be in competition for students and philanthropic dollars. How do you set the table for establishing collaboration among this diversity of potentially competing interests? The answer is to identify a shared essential question.

Two aspects of the question mattered in our story. We asked: *How might we support rabbinical and cantorial students to grow as innovative leaders who are able to engage meaningfully in our rapidly changing world?*

First, the question posed was vital to all the potential participants. Regardless of religious orientation, the world has changed for all of us. "We are *all* invested in building the Jewish community and training outstanding Jewish leaders with the skills they need to be successful," says Amanda Shechter, executive director at Yeshivat Maharat and an active participant in the collaboration. "We all know the Jewish community is changing and the skills from the past will not be sufficient. This recognition transcends denomination."

While the question we posed spoke to needs across denominations, it also never required participants to compromise or abandon their unique values or affiliation. Coming together can't mean diminishing one's values or identity. According to Dr. Ora Horn Prouser, CEO and academic dean of the Academy for Jewish Religion (AJR), New York, an inter-seminary participant, everyone is able to say, "We always felt respected. The process was inclusive." Rabbi Jan Katzew, director of the rabbinical program at HUC-JIR Cincinnati echoes that sentiment: "We were not asked to give up who we are."

Second, the presenting question that generated our shared work was intentionally framed with the phrase, *"How might we,"* as recommended by proponents of Design Thinking. This opening phrase signals possibility and cues a need for collective action.

An astonishing thing happened when reaching out to a list of rabbinical school leaders we thought might be interested in the project. Everyone we asked said yes. Since our first gathering, hosted by Rabbi Stephanie Ruskay at the Jewish Theological Seminary, our numbers have grown. And they continue to grow.

Identifying a question that speaks to all needs while never asking individuals or organizations to abandon their core identities enabled success. Common need and respecting differences is essential. As Lisa Grant says, "The challenges of disruption are affecting the entire Jewish world. We were able to come together around our similarities and our differences."

To set the table for collaboration amidst diversity, identify an essential shared question, respect one another's differences and humbly acknowledge no one has the answers yet. Don't just signal that each voice is important. Really mean it.

3. Insist on Appreciative Inquiry

To actualize the intention of truly honoring each voice in service of generating collective action, the inter-seminary collaboration used practices prescribed by proponents of Appreciative Inquiry (AI). AI practitioners inquire into the best of what already exists in order to light the way to the future. Our AI agendas invited everyone at our gatherings to share something their school had already tried. We used AI questions like, "Share a time when you were wildly successful," "If you had three wishes what would they be?" and "What would it have looked like if the thing you had tried had worked?"

Everyone had something to teach. Fondly, I remember a meeting at HUC–JIR's New York campus hosted by Grant and Dr. Evie Rotstein, when each person around the large conference table jotted down someone else's ideas. Everyone had something to learn. Trust grew.

We were buoyed by what we learned each school had been doing. Trust in one another continued to grow. Yet we recognized the limitations of the wisdom in the room.

So, we invited innovation leaders to teach us. Experts in the field, such as Rabbi Sid Schwarz of the Clergy Leadership Incubator and Rabbi George Wielechowski, then of the Open Dor Project, generously volunteered to teach us about the existing ecosystem that is supporting clergy-as-innovation-leaders.

At one session, an innovation leader suggested that the skills we were exploring could *only* be learned once students became professionals in the field. We struggled with that notion, asking what mindsets and skills students might cultivate as foundational prior to graduation. At a gathering hosted by YCT, an AI approach provided an answer. We shared numerous stories about students who were already learning and acting as intra- and entrepreneurs. An inspiring picture emerged, leading us to embrace a shared belief that students couldn't afford to wait until they graduated to cultivate their ability to lead as innovators.

Collaboration across organizations has the potential to devolve in numerous ways. By using positive structures for gatherings, such as agendas infused with AI practices, you can avoid common pitfalls like posturing or negativity. Optimism and glimpses of what's possible are jet fuel for collaboration across difference.

4. Drive Without Money

Our collaboration has operated for almost three years funded solely by the currency of shared need, honoring our differences and growing trust. The drive to find answers to our questions and good will—not the agendas of funders—has kept us moving forward.

Without outside funding, we have and continue to sustain the collaboration with a spirit of volunteerism. Participant leaders set agendas, facilitate sections of learning, host gatherings, and reach out to new potential partners. We also learned that we needed to identify a "backbone:" an organization concept derived from Collective Impact that promotes a social change approach to bringing multiple organizations together to address a shared issue. The backbone ensures that an initiative stays focused and moves forward—even without funding.

For this project, I volunteered to act as the backbone. This work fell into the scope of my job. As vice president of innovation and impact at Reconstructing Judaism, I am empowered to work with partners to seek solutions to tough challenges and to uncover wondrous unseen opportunities in the Jewish community. And, to be fully transparent, I was also driven to find a shared solution, because I had taught the social entrepreneurship course twice previously and wasn't satisfied. I needed help.

Sustaining collaboration without funding over a long period of time is challenging. As interested as participants were in our shared question, everyone has limited bandwidth and has to prioritize where to spend time. Without the promise of funding or direct benefits to one's school, one would expect momentum to wane.

To convey a full picture, I need to share that although moving forward without funding can be challenging, one participant spoke of feeling grateful that we didn't have it. "We naturally drove our collaboration where we wanted it to go without having to meet the goals of someone with a check."

It is a testament to the spirit of the group that everyone stayed involved without the scaffolding or promise of funding. Today, as a result of our shared drive, funding is actually materializing.

Don't wait until a funder gives you a green light or sets their agenda as your own. Generate momentum out of the will of individuals addressing a critical shared need. Get a backbone and expect everyone to roll up their sleeves in search of answers they really need.

5. Move to Action—Attract Resources

By the summer of 2018, after numerous productive gatherings, we were ready for action. Rabbi Elan Babchuck was our guest teacher and began his session by asking us an innovator's question: "What is the pain point of the schools?" Horn Prouser spoke in our collective voice that had emerged over time: "We don't want a disconnect between the creativity and imagination of our students and what they can make real in the world."

Babchuck, a spiritual entrepreneur who lives what he teaches, generously offered a way forward, volunteering without hesitation the full resources of the Glean Network and Clal. What inspired him to this offering? As he says of his own commitment and the motivation of spiritual innovators, it stems from "a moment of obligation which is a time in your life when you have seen an opportunity or problem and you feel called to do something."

Since that time, Babchuck and his team have been working with us to design an online synchronous course to meet the shared and unique needs of students across time zones and perspectives. As one might suspect, meeting everyone's needs has been challenging.

A number of the school leaders reported that the hardest part of the entire collaboration has been logistics. Differing accreditation requirements, tuition structures, and calendars were just a few of those complex logistical challenges. Babchuck modeled an entrepreneurial approach, listening carefully to everyone's needs and responding with flexibility. Initially, for example, the course was to have one section offered on Monday afternoons. Calls by Babchuck to each school leader changed that. Babchuck modeled flexibility and now the course is being offered in three sections at three different times.

At the date of this writing, we are ready to launch. We expect glitches. We'll surely be cycling through a test-learn feedback loop that will provide insight into our shared question. I believe we have enough trust to manage them as they come. As Peretz reminds us, "Collaboration is a greater value than perfection." We know that no single school could have created this alone.

One-and-a-half years since Babchuck began working with us, additional funding has materialized. In my role as backbone, I've worked with Reconstructing Judaism to secure monies to support student projects created in the course. To everyone's delight, we now have funding to expand RRC's innovation grant program to students at other rabbinical seminaries as well. Students from across seminaries will now be able to apply for a number of ignition grants and a $20,000 2:1 launch grant for a project. Working in partnership with Babchuck, we've also received a grant to support a retreat for students and possibly one for a gathering of the collaboration's leadership. Babchuck continues to seek funding to support this gathering of participants as well as possible additional grant-funding expansion.

The deans and professors of schools in this project have all expressed interest in building on what we have started. We know this course is only a start. It is going to teach us a lot. And we are most grateful that funding is now coming as a result of our shared commitment and vision.

To be an effective collaboration, not just a group of people with diverse perspectives called to a conference table, it is essential to invest in building trust, common purpose, and optimism. Only then can you grow the safe and generative climate for people across difference to take risks with inventive action that attract valuable resources and funding to enact a shared vision.

Conclusion

Our inter-seminary initiative has taken advantage of the Jewish community's emerging culture for collaboration by using five power tools: get out of your own space; identify a shared question that honors differences; insist on appreciative inquiry; drive without funding; and move to action—attract resources. We've grown to believe that the answer to our initial question includes our students learning innovation tools *and*, just as importantly, learning and working across perspectives. *Leading Through Innovation* students will learn and apply innovation tools to address needs in their communities. They will practice the power tools of collaboration across difference, helping each other to create solutions that no singular person or organization could ever achieve. Now is the time to take advantage of our emerging culture of collaboration.

Participants in the Inter-seminary collaboration:

Academy for Jewish Religion, New York
Academy for Jewish Religion California
ALEPH Rabbinical Program
Hebrew College
Hebrew Union College–Jewish Institute of Religion, New York
Hebrew Union College–Jewish Institute of Religion, Cincinnati
The Jewish Theological Seminary
Leo Baeck College, London
Reconstructionist Rabbinical College
Yeshiva University
Yeshivat Chovevei Torah
Yeshivat Maharat
Ziegler School of Rabbinic Studies, American Jewish University

Epilogue

Our course launched in Spring 2020. Deans and professors in our inter-seminary initiative kindly, generously, and thoughtfully express appreciation for the time spent together and for what we are creating. They made time for sharing reflections and insights on this collaborative experience in order to inform this writing.

What impact will our efforts have on our students? We wish for them, as Horn Prouser says, "To have the collegial relationships across organizations. We know that is so important to them." This wish is starting to be fulfilled.

Prior to the course beginning, students were invited to make a "virtual coffee date" with a student from a different school. Bena, a student at AJR in New York had "virtual coffee" with an AJRCA student and an HUC New York student. Following the meetings, she emailed Rabbi Babchuck to express, "Because of your first assignment, I had the pleasure of meeting and having *wonderful* conversations with two people from two different seminaries. In each case, we felt that we formed a connection to build on throughout the Entrepreneurship class, as well as a foundation for a distance friendship, perhaps even beyond the classroom. And for that, I wish to say thank you." Patiently, yet with great anticipation, we'll have to see if Bena's experience is a sign of things to come.

Part 5:

Communities

A Return to the Transdenominational Cantor
Lisa Peicott

The role of the cantor has been, and rightly should be, transdenominational. Limiting cantors to a single denominational affiliation is both ahistorical and, I would argue, goes against the essential function of the *hazzan* (cantor) as a *sheliach tzibbur*, an emissary, and leader for the Jewish people—not just a particular group of Jewish people. For cantors, sectarian divides are actually a recent phenomenon and, thanks to the pioneering work of female cantors and their influence on synagogue music, will likely soon be seen as a temporary aberration in the long, transdenominational history of the cantorate. Based on my own experience transitioning between different denominations as a cantor, I am convinced that this change—already well underway in practice—is the best and only practical way forward for the future of cantorial training and education, as well as the best way to serve the Jewish people.

My mother is the daughter of a Holocaust survivor. My father was raised as a nondenominational Christian. Upon marrying, they agreed that their future children would be raised exclusively Jewish. Growing up, my younger brother, David, and I attended services at Temple Aliyah, a Conservative synagogue where I became bat mitzvah. At temple, I became well-versed in traditional liturgy. I loved *hazzanut* (cantorial artistry) from an early age, but my family was like many others in the Conservative movement: quietly non-traditional in our home practice. We did not keep kosher or observe Shabbat regularly. I never knew that the fall holidays continued on after Yom Kippur; my family never observed them. Despite my upbringing, I did not feel particularly connected to the Conservative movement itself. I considered myself "Just Jewish," a theme that would take me through my adult life and into my career as a cantor.

And so, when I applied to the Academy for Jewish Religion California (AJRCA) at the age of twenty-seven, I was pleased by the pluralistic curriculum. Having the opportunity to learn Reform, Conservative, and even Orthodox liturgy and theology alongside colleagues who represented the range of Judaism fit my personal identity of "Just Jewish." At the start of my journey at AJRCA, I was unsure where I would ultimately land in the Jewish world. But I knew I wanted to serve Jews—not serve a movement.

During orientation at AJRCA, we went around the room and each incoming student recited their Jewish self-history. I was surrounded by those brought up Orthodox, Reform, Conservative, Reconstructionist, Renewal, secular humanist, and everywhere in between—all eager to learn alongside one another. But no matter our personal upbringing, we all wanted to serve Jews. Often, outsiders would wonder, "How can you all study together, if you all believe different things?" To this I responded, "You know the joke: 'Two Jews, three opinions.'" In AJRCA classrooms I learned that the role of the cantor is to minister to all Jews, not just those who agree with our own religious or philosophical viewpoints.

During my first year at AJRCA, I began serving as the cantorial intern at a prominent Conservative synagogue in West Los Angeles. I was daily learning the ins and outs of the movement, leading services, teaching classes, and officiating at lifecycle events. At the same time, I was working as a cantorial soloist at a large Reform congregation, where I led services and holiday celebrations. My pluralistic education gave me the tools to move seamlessly between two ostensibly different congregations—and I quickly realized they were not so different from one another. Both temples were filled with people excited to genuinely connect and be moved by our ancient traditions. In my experience, these congregants tended not to narrowly define themselves based on *halakhic* (legal) stringencies or the phrasing of a mission statement. They were Jews who wanted to incorporate religious customs and rituals into their lives. My transdenominational skills as a cantorial student were put to the test. I came to understand that my primary role was not to uphold strict denominational guidelines and restrictions, but rather to facilitate Jewish experiences and connections through music—a role that cantors have fulfilled and interpreted for centuries.

The basic foundation of any Jewish service is liturgy, which is broken down into a set or *matbeah* of prayers affixed to certain times and certain days. The sound of each prayer can be reduced further to a system called *nusach*, which applies a prescribed set of scales and melodies for each prayer. Despite much of Jewish liturgy remaining the same throughout the year, the *nusach* ensures that a daily service sounds different than a Shabbat service, a morning service sounds different than an evening service or holiday, and so on. In theory, one could be dropped into any Ashkenazi synagogue and, just by hearing the cantor's voice, know which service is taking place. Whether one is Reform, Orthodox, or any denomination (or nondenomination) in between, the purpose of *nusach* remains the same. That said, different melodies are used across regions, geographic locations, and even neighboring temples—and many liberal congregations do not adhere very closely to *nusach* at all. Nevertheless, the fundamental basis of the Jewish prayer service for all denominations is, explicitly or hidden somewhere in the sonic fabric, a musical mode of prayer employed throughout the centuries.

The role of the cantor came to prominence out of the need for a leader to interpret these musical modes and pray out loud for the congregation. As the demand for public prayer increased within the diaspora, the role of the *hazzan* grew in importance. Many congregations were led by a sole *hazzan* who would lead the service and officiate at lifecycle events, while the historical rabbi was concerned with questions regarding Jewish law. Following the devastation of World War II and the near annihilation of European Jewry, American philanthropists realized that professional schools were vital to train future generations of American cantors. Congregations that hired cantors often brought them in from Europe. An American training program would ensure religious continuity and professional standards for years to come. While rabbinic seminaries had been ordaining rabbis since the late nineteenth century, the American Jewish movements knew that they must regroup and professionalize the cantorate. The Reform movement's School of Sacred Music of the Hebrew Union College–Jewish Institute of Religion (HUC) was founded in 1948, originally to train cantors of *klal yisrael*—all stripes. Shortly thereafter, the Conservative Cantors Institute of the Jewish Theological Seminary (JTS) was founded in 1952 and the Orthodox Cantorial Training Institute of Yeshiva University followed in 1954. With the advent of formal training programs, cantors were admitted to professional unions and joined congregations affiliated with denominations. Cantors became pivotal figures within these movements and were no longer mostly temporary laborers, itinerant performers, or independent contractors hired by temples to conduct prayer services. Despite the historical role of the cantor as a transdenominational figure, the creation of formal training institutions corralled the cantor into a single denominational box for several decades. But all that would soon change.

Whether one chooses to attend JTS, HUC, or a transdenominational program, there are four main professional organizations that cantors can join: The Cantors Assembly, associated with the Conservative Movement; the American Conference of Cantors, associated with the Reform movement; the Guild of Temple Musicians, a union of cantors, soloists, choir directors, music educators, instrumentalists, and composers affiliated with the American Conference of Cantors; and the Women Cantors Network, which is unaffiliated. While graduation from JTS or HUC guarantees admission into their respective organization, non-affiliated clergy and clergy from outside movements are now able to test into an organization with a written exam and oral audition. Many cantors, like me, belong to multiple professional organizations, attend yearly conferences, regional meetings, educational seminars, and share music and best practices with colleagues across the denominational spectrum. Aside from just belonging to different professional organizations, there are many cantors who, based on job availability and geographical preference, are currently serving congregations that differ from their original ordination. With the overall decline of synagogue membership across the country, many small synagogues are closing down or being incorporated into larger congregations. There are simply not enough congregational jobs available for each respective movement's graduates, resulting in cantors being called upon to serve at congregations of various denominations and un-affiliated institutions. The reality of the job landscape forces cantors to reevaluate their role as Jewish clergy. With the decline in the denominational job market, cantors, out of necessity, are returning to the historical model of the *hazzan* serving the spiritual and religious needs of all Jews.

I happen to be one of those cantors who has gained experience at congregations of various affiliations. My first pulpit was at a Conservative temple, where I served as the *hazzan sheni* (second cantor), as well as the temple's ritual director. In addition to leading services, teaching, and chaplaincy, I oversaw the twice-daily *minyan* (quorum) and maintained ritual items, ensuring that the temple lived up to the strictures of Jewish law. The combination of my pluralistic education and familiarity with Conservative practice allowed me to fulfill this role despite not being trained in a Conservative program. While the rabbis at this synagogue received an education within the movement, both the senior cantor and I had been ordained by AJRCA, a transdenominational program. Despite our pluralistic backgrounds, we were able to fit comfortably within the clergy dynamic and contribute to the spiritual experience of the community.

After a year on the pulpit, my cantorial journey next took me to one of the largest Reform congregations in the country (now unaffiliated). My exposure to Reform liturgy, music, and theology throughout my education at AJRCA, as well as my soloist work, prepared me for this rather significant transition. In liturgy class, I studied the Reform movement's *mahzorim* and *siddurim* (prayer books), and was expected to know classical *hazzanut* as well as contemporary settings of prayers in the Reform movement. I needed to know it all in order to serve any congregation or *minyan* that came my way.

How difficult is it to transition between two different synagogues representing two denominations? On paper, the two movements have distinct theological models, practices, customs, and very different views regarding the place of Jewish law in everyday life. However, lately, the aforementioned musical cross-fertilization has eased the way for transitioning from one to the other. This cross-fertilization, seen in the last four decades, can be attributed largely to the modern addition of women cantors to the *bimah* (pulpit), and their culture-changing influence on the music of the synagogue for all progressive denominations. Their presence has accelerated the breakdown of the denominational divide for cantors, and has restored the cantorate to its traditional transdenominational role.

When Barbara Ostfeld was invested by HUC in 1975, she became the first officially recognized female cantor. While women on the West Coast, such as Cantor Perryne Anker, associate dean of AJRCA's cantorial school, had been working as a soloist and cantor for many years, Ostfeld was the first woman to be certified by an academic institution. Following graduation, Ostfeld found placement and was admitted to the American Conference of Cantors (ACC), which had been the gathering place for Reform male cantors since 1953. Almost a decade later, the Jewish Theological Seminary invested its first female cantorial graduates, Erica Lippitz and Marla Rosenfeld Barugel. Despite their full acceptance and ordination from the Cantors Institute, the Cantors Assembly did not accept these women as members until 1991. For the few women ordained by the Reform movement, the ACC was a "boy's club" they could partake in, but did not fully accept them. Women invested by the Conservative movement were completely barred from professional membership, and thus had no professional support. While these women had broken the glass ceiling of the synagogue, the cantorate was still essentially a career for men in a religious system dictated by men. The music of the synagogue was overwhelmingly written by men and meant to be interpreted by male voices. It was only through joining forces that women were able to break that barrier and, in the process of doing so, break the divide that had separated cantors since the establishment of professional training programs.

Cantor Deborah Katchko-Zimmerman, the granddaughter of the illustrious Cantor Adolph Katchko, formed the Women's Cantors Network (WCN) in 1981. A traditionally trained cantor, Deborah felt isolated from her male counterparts. She founded the WCN as an outreach and educational support network for female cantors of all denominations. Through the years, it was a place where women of various backgrounds and affiliations could learn and collaborate together. They created a newsletter and annual conference, and by the 1990s the network had grown to ninety cantors and soloists. As more and more women entered the cantorate, the barrier of denominations separating cantors was permanently breached, and the crossfertilization of music, educational conferences, and collaborations infiltrated the denominations. While each movement continues to have their annual conventions, there are also conferences in which affiliated and non-affiliated cantors from across the country unite. Denominational allegiance (or non-allegiance) is left at the door as we gather together as Jewish cantors whose shared mission is to use the power of music and melody to serve the Jewish people. In addition to closing gaps between denominations by encouraging the cross-fertilization of practices across the profession, women cantors have, through their physical presence on the *bimah*, effectively changed the music of the American cantorate. The physiological differences between male and female voices have given way to a new sound of the American cantorate, one that has been widely accepted by most male and female cantors, further decreasing the gap between progressive denominations and enabling cantors to serve a variety of Jewish communities.

In his article, "Why Can't a Woman Chant Like a Man?," Cantor William Sharlin (z"l) compared this question to the authenticity of Bach's keyboard music being played on a modern piano:

> *Hazzanut*, that vital musical heritage of our people, did, after all, develop its uniqueness out of the vocal distinctiveness and character of the male singer—the tenor no less. With a Bach prelude and fugue, one might argue that its musical substance is of such pure abstractness, that it loses nothing of its essence when played on a modern keyboard (many even say Bach would have eagerly accepted a well-tempered Steinway Grand). But with *hazzanut* the simple transference from male to female voice is a difficult matter. The very heart of *hazzanut*—the indescribable earthiness, texture, taste, and pathos in need of a wide range of color and primitive-like ornamentation, deeply linked with the spontaneity of a male-davening congregation, chanted in a language that was almost exclusively reserved for men—should naturally and necessarily be bound up in the male voice.[1]

---

[1] William Sharlin, "Why Can't a Woman Chant Like a Man?," in *Jewish Sacred Music and Jewish Identity: Continuity and Fragmentation*, ed. Jonathan L. Friedmann

His argument is not that women are unable to chant like men, because, as we can hear in recordings of Bathsheba and other *khazantes* (female "cantor impersonators") of the early to mid-twentieth century, women could chant like men (in their chest voice) and could imitate them quite convincingly. What Sharlin proposes is that women should not be *expected* to imitate the male instrument, as they have the ability to bring their own vocal uniqueness and timbre to cantorial music. Sharlin stresses that what is most important in *hazzanut* is the sincerity of expression and genuine engagement in worship. In the end, it is the person who touches the congregant, not the baritone, contralto, tenor or soprano; and when that authenticity through voice is reached, that is what makes a singer a *hazzan*. With the entrance of women into the cantorate, there has been a movement away from the *hazzanut* of "Golden Age" compositions. Instead, women have embraced their unique vocal instruments and have helped to create a new world of synagogue song that has spread across liberal Judaism.

The reinvention of American synagogue music was greatly influenced by the folk music revival of the 1960s and further strengthened by the presence of women entering the cantorate. The folk song, a tradition that exists in all musical cultures, became increasingly associated with its American usage, as with the works of such singers as Bob Dylan, Joni Mitchell, Joan Baez, and Peter, Paul, and Mary. These musicians used song as a vehicle for political activism, and accompanied themselves on guitar to entertain large audiences. They created a sense of shared spiritual experience through their music, and this combination of music and performance soon found its way into the synagogue. Young musical innovators in the Reform movement, like Debbie Friedman, desired a new sound that would reflect their Jewish identities—balancing traditional values and the modern American mainstream. They turned away from the music language of their home synagogues, which was dominated by choirs and the classical repertoire of male *hazzanim*, and composed new settings for group singing with guitar accompaniment.

The music of Debbie Friedman and other feminist pioneers was emotional and personal. Just like the *hazzanut* of Yossele Rosenblatt

and Brad Stetson (St. Paul, MN: Paragon House, 2008), 96.

in his day and age, it spoke to the Jewish people. Specifically, it spoke to women, who were finding their own spiritual voices, both on the pulpit and in the pews. Not only did the music of Debbie Friedman challenge musical conventions, such as the aforementioned *nusach*, but it also challenged the masculine language found in Jewish liturgy, which was created *by* men *for* men. By introducing gender-neutral language, it became a more authentic prayer expression for many female cantors. This music transformed Jewish liturgy by re-conceptualizing its meaning and structure. Just as the choral music of Salomon Sulzer and Louis Lewandowski reinvented European synagogue music during the nineteenth century, the folk settings of Debbie Friedman and other female composers re-envisioned what Jewish liturgy could sound like and who could sing it, particularly in the liberal movements.

Perhaps inevitably, this new music faced criticism—particularly among male Reform and Conservative cantors—for not being written in the traditional modes (*nusach*). Women cantors (and the congregations they served) proved more accepting. The opening of the cantorate to women and their willingness to incorporate contemporary music into their repertoires allowed for the creation of a new American *nusach*, which is now widely accepted in all progressive synagogues. Despite the initial resistance of male cantors, the power of this new music spoke for itself, and has since spread to *bimot* across the country—and the globe.

These melodies transcend denominational divides and are not only a beloved part of the musical liturgy, but also an integral sound of the American cantorate. Men and women have continued to expand their musical vocabularies, ushering in new styles influenced by the surrounding secular world. Whether one is a student at a transdenominational program or a denominationally affiliated school, it is a requirement to incorporate these new music genres into one's cantorate. The presence of female cantors, and their need to find their own unique voices, has changed the sound of the cantorate, uniting the denominations through a new musical language and expression of our ancient text.

There are very important questions that must be addressed by individuals pursuing a pluralistic path within the Jewish world. While being able to serve as clergy for any congregation certainly reflects the historical model of the cantor, the role of the cantor cannot simply be reduced to the practicality of leading services. While singing and chanting remain a major part of the job description, the role of the cantor is increasingly like that of the rabbi—a communal spiritual leader and teacher. While many cantors have the ability to navigate the liturgy, theology, and music of the various progressive denominations (and nondenominations), each cantor must be aware of what is at the core of their own Judaism. Within each denomination and each synagogue there is a foundation of belief and interpretation of our tradition. With the scarcity of jobs and the necessity to move between denominational settings, those of us with a pluralistic background need to not only "talk the talk" of being a cantor, but also authentically "walk the walk" of each congregation we lead.

A pluralistic education is a choice, and perhaps not the right choice for everyone, partly due to challenges like these. A transdenominational education is based on the tenets of the *etz chayim* (tree of life). The trunk of the tree is our core values as Jews, which I define as a belief in one God, the wisdom of Torah, and that human beings have a responsibility to make the world a better place. The branches of the tree represent many different denominations and spiritual paths that exist within Judaism. With a pluralistic education, we are taught the core, but we are also given the choice of many paths to take. Do we choose our paths based on what a congregation can offer us or our need of employment, or do we live the values of our authentic Jewish selves within the denominational system? Does a Reform cantor become *shomer Shabbat* or ritually observant to work within a traditional model? Does a Conservative Cantor give up observance to work in a Reconstructionist community? Or does each clergy member have to draw a sacred fence around their own practices? We live in a society that is full of labels. Pluralism gives cantors a chance to explore deeply and, perhaps for the first time, their authentic "Just Jewish" self.

A Case Study in Nondenominational Judaism
Yocheved Mintz

A small community of fewer than one hundred family units, Congregation P'nai Tikvah was established as Valley Outreach Congregation in 1994. An offshoot of the synagogue of the same name in the Los Angeles area, the founding rabbi, Richard Shachet (*z"l*) brought together a diverse group of people primarily from the west side of Las Vegas and Henderson, Nevada. The congregation was loosely affiliated with the Reconstructionist denomination, and Rabbi Shachet was involved in the Renewal movement. It soon became evident, however, that the majority of congregants not only did not know what Reconstructionist Judaism meant, but did not seem to care.

The congregation met only once a month, and services frequently involved guest entertainers. There was a cantor (with a sketchy background) and a small children's education program, but no formal classes for adults. In 2004, the rabbi announced his retirement, conducted a rabbinic search, and approached me to take over the congregation.

It would be my first congregation, having been a member of the second graduating class of the Academy for Jewish Religion California. What I found was challenging. I spent the first few months establishing a proper 501(c)(3) status for the synagogue, which had never been completed, and setting up an acceptable financial system—as, it turned out, the books had actually been intermingled with those of the founding rabbi.

In addition to reorganizing the business side of the synagogue, we increased services to twice a month, meeting on the first and third Friday night, and had twice-monthly Torah study on Shabbat mornings as well. This increase in substance was met with varying degrees of acceptance and/or push-back. The congregation had come to expect a certain amount of entertainment from the services and, evidently, very little, if any, intellectual challenge. Reconstructionist Judaism, sometimes called "the thinking person's Judaism," encouraged thought, study, and discussion. This did not sit well with some, but was embraced by others. Transitioning from homemade service booklets to the Reconstructionist prayer book, *Kol HaNeshama*, was welcomed, although we then received complaints about there being too much Hebrew. (Of course, we also got complaints that there was not enough Hebrew.)

Still, for the most part, the congregation remained somewhat steady, until shortly before Rosh Hashanah following the first year of my tenure as the community's rabbi. It turns out that, although the founding rabbi had hand-picked me to succeed him, and had, in fact, actually moved out of town, ostensibly retiring to Portland, Oregon, he stayed in contact with several members of the congregation's task force (board) and had, without informing me, decided he was coming back to form a *chavurah* (fellowship) with those members who would follow him. I discovered this only after the tragic event that nearly tore the congregation apart. Evidently, Rabbi Shachet was en route to Las Vegas to conduct the new *chavurah*'s first Rosh Hashanah service when he was in a fatal automobile accident. The shock of his death was felt throughout the community. My presence at the *shiva* was awkward; those who had surreptitiously been planning to be a part of the new *chavurah* could not look me in the eye. Nevertheless, I assured everyone that they were welcome at our Yamim Ha-Noraim services. The *chavurah* floundered and never really got off the ground, but the damage had been done. We lost about a third of the congregation. Ironically, had the founding rabbi notified me that he wanted to return, I would have welcomed him as the rabbi emeritus and would have loved to work with him. (*Tovim ha-sh'naim min ha-echad*—two are better than one.) But that, unfortunately was not to be. Over the years, a handful of families did rejoin the congregation, but we have not recouped the numbers we initially had.

Another challenge was the venue in which we would meet. From the congregation's inception, it was considered a congregation "without walls." Within the first few months of my taking over, the community center where we met had tripled the rent and we had to seek another venue. Over the ensuing years, we moved from place to place, renting from three different church groups and a Jewish mortuary. Each place had its own challenges—one with poor lighting in the parking lot, one with a not-too-subtle antisemitic attitude, one which we simply outgrew, and one whose interfaith involvement was wonderful but whose actual physical space was simply deemed too open and, therefore, too vulnerable to possible attack. All of this brought us to our current home, the beautiful *bet midrash* (study hall) of the Adelson Educational Campus, a safe, attractive, and welcoming Jewish institution. With each move, as expected, we lost some members and gained new members; but, ultimately, we remained at essentially the same size that we had been reduced to following the unfortunate breakaway situation when the founding rabbi had decided to return.

A challenge we had not anticipated turned out to be our very name: Valley Outreach Synagogue. After several years, we realized that people were confused by the word "outreach" and interpreted it as an LGBTQI+ community or Jews for Jesus. While we are certainly welcoming to all, we are definitely Jewish, so we polled our congregation and decided to change our name to Congregation P'nai Tikvah (faces of hope) in order clarify that we were indeed a Jewish community.

The concept of Jewish community was in and of itself somewhat challenging. When I first came to Las Vegas in the late 1990s, one could say that we had a growing Jewish population, but referring to it as "community" would not have been accurate. It was fragmented, siloed, and, to a great extent, not self-identifying. Over the ensuing twenty-plus years, however, a Jewish community has evolved, but it is still uniquely "Las Vegas," consisting of a preponderance of people who have come from other cities. It is estimated that less than 6% of the Jewish population of Las Vegas is affiliated with synagogues. Our congregation would serve a small subset of that small percentage.

Yet another challenge turned out to be our affiliation with the Reconstructionist denomination. We had been paying dues to the Reconstructionist Rabbinical Assembly and the Reconstructionist organization; we had invested in Reconstructionist *siddurim* (prayer books); and we had been marketing the congregation as the only Reconstructionist congregation in Nevada; but we were not growing significantly. It was helpful to people who were looking for a Reconstructionist congregation, but those who were not familiar with Reconstructionism did not really care about the congregation's affiliation or philosophy.

And there were problems with our relationship with the Reconstructionist movement itself. Our affiliation was decidedly one-sided, and we needed help—which was not forthcoming. A little more background: Members of the congregation came from the full range of denominations, and those who attended services enjoyed them. We used every opportunity to teach and elevate the spirit through *kavanot* (intentions). We used music, sang, and embodied parts of the service through dance; the warm, welcoming atmosphere of the community also attracted multi-faith families. But, although we offered adult education, youth education (Jewlicious Learning and Teen Torah Tribe), pastoral counseling, and we accompanied our members through all of the lifecycle moments, we have never been large enough to afford to pay the clergy staff (rabbi and cantor) acceptable wages. We have been serving an underserved segment of the community, as we wanted to make our services affordable to all. We found that we received essentially the same income by moving to a self-determined pledge system, rather than a sliding scale dues membership policy. But we needed to triple the size of the congregation in order to offer a living wage for the clergy. So, I went to the powers that be in the Reconstructionist organization. We sought guidance and assistance so we could grow. First one, then another, consultant was sent, hope was raised, promises were made, but there was never any follow-up. In fact, the consultants themselves were let go. Perhaps the timing was off, as the denominational institutions (including Reform, Conservative, and Reconstructionist) were in disarray and in the midst of years of reorganizing. The bottom line was that help did not come and, ultimately, realizing that there was no return on our investment in the denominational organization, our board decided to discontinue affiliation.

Has there been any effect on the congregation? Thus far, I cannot see much effect either positive or negative on the congregation, although I imagine that the fact that we are saving the cost of affiliation might be considered a positive. Whatever benefit might result from affiliation was lost when it disappointed us by not being there to help guide us for growth when we needed it.

Was I prepared to "go it alone"? My studies at the Academy for Jewish Religion California had been transdenominational in scope. My personal background was an experience in all the various movements. My own spiritual practice is progressive, but I am comfortable in any synagogue setting that accepts me as a rabbi. The transdenominational reality of Congregation P'nai Tikvah is a fact, although most people still think of us as Reconstructionist with Renewal influence.

At this point in time, Congregation P'nai Tikvah is in a safe and welcoming venue. We continue to offer adult and youth education. We share each other's homes for Rosh Chodesh, social events, and Torah study. We continue to gather anywhere from twenty to seventy people for Kabbalat Shabbat and Shabbat Maariv services, and we remain hopeful that we will grow our membership. But the paradigm of synagogue affiliation with the denominational institutions seems to be shifting. What our parents and grandparents took as a given— membership in a *shul*—seems to be shifting as well. Rabbi Zalman Schachter-Shalomi (z"*l*), anticipated this and spoke extensively of this as a major paradigm shift, but he himself never wanted the Renewal movement he founded to become a Movement (with a capital "M"). What has remained constant is the need for community and the need for spiritual sustenance, but whether they will continue to come from traditional prayer-based, service-driven, denomination-affiliated congregations seems more and more unlikely.

Recovery Judaism: Principles of Living T'shuvah
Igaël Gurin-Malous

Eilu v'eilu— "*These* and *these* are the living words of *God*" (אלו ואלו דברי אלוהים חיים)—from Talmud Bavli, Eruvin 13b, has been a guiding principle in Jewish life since the creation of rabbinical Judaism. The value of debate and pluralism (not just tolerance) has been at the core of our religion and culture for generations. It is what has made us stronger and more adaptable as a nation, and has been a source of refuge to all those who seek to be seen where previously they would have been shunned or hidden. Expanding our ring of inclusion further to those who suffer from addiction is part of our generation's challenge.

Seeking to create a platform of support and education to all those who suffer, including their families and communities, I have tried to articulate principles of recovery that can help us invite, include, and better understand those among us who are in pain and want to be part of recovery Judaism. This is a nondenominational and nonjudgmental approach, embracing all, regardless of background or affiliation.

With so many people suffering, and in so much pain, in addiction, mental anguish, and spiritual poverty, how can Judaism adapt to offer relief and direction? How can we create intentional communities of healing, recovery, and meaning in our modern era? Why do so many religious institutions fail to inspire, heal, and protect those who need it the most? Just as Abraham Joshua Heschel spoke in 1963 of a moral emergency, we are facing our own moral emergency as we enter the third decade of the twenty-first century, because we have failed to embrace those who suffer in our midst.

Recovery Judaism enables us to see those who step bravely into the light with authenticity, courage, and dignity. Living T'shuvah is not a single act of repentance but rather is a daily act of living in truth, repair, and strength. Recovery Judaism offers a covenant of understanding and a method of recognizing and accepting the multidimensionality of the human condition. To those who previously would suffer in isolation and loneliness, recovery Judaism promises to embrace and connect all of us. Only through these principles can we be true to the words of our ancestors: "All of Israel is responsible for one another."

Living T'shuvah

The Hebrew term *t'shuvah* translates to a few different words and ideas: repentance, return, and an answer. Together, they form a dynamic bond that requires us to examine our actions and their consequences, thus allowing us to learn and grow. Repentance denotes our ability to change and develop, while return implies coming back to oneself. The solace of our pain begins in our awareness of it; the awareness triggers a change in our action so that we may grow and find our way back to a better state of self.

Living T'shuvah is not a novel idea; it is embedded in our traditional teachings.

Talmud Bavli, Shabbat 153a, teaches:

> We learned there in a *mishna* that Rabbi Eliezer says: *T'shuva* one day before your death. Rabbi Eliezer's students asked him: But does a person know the day on which he will die? He said to them: All the more so this is a good piece of advice, and one should do *t'shuva* today lest he die tomorrow; and by following this advice one will spend his entire life in a state of *t'shuva*.

King Solomon also said wisely: "At all times your clothes should be white, and oil shall not be absent from upon your head" (Ecclesiastes 9:8), meaning that a person always needs to be prepared.

Disconnect and Moral Urgency

There are meaningful questions, but who can be trusted to provide us with answers? These questions often plague us when we are young and continue as we grow older, but as the grind of everyday life takes hold, we bury them deep in our minds. Perhaps years later, when we read a book or get to know someone special, we may feel for a moment, an hour, an evening, our place in the universe, our purpose in life, and recognize our need for connection and authenticity. We may gain some insight and feel good for a bit, but then we return to our daily life and it is lost.

We have become so used to playing the role that we have crafted for ourselves that we lose our ability to connect to our real emotions, appreciate their complexities, or even feel them at all. If we do feel them and they are "too much," we do whatever we can to drown them out. Most of us go through life like this, not really paying attention to the erosion of our selves. We sacrifice who we want to be for the sake of who we think we need to be.

Modern society has turned the human condition into a pathology. Our experiences, both shared and unique, have become sources of ailment, anguish, or torment. Life is a battlefield, we are told. The cities we live in are concrete jungles, we learn. Life has become a fight. We now describe our experiences, our emotions, as diseases that need to be cured—trauma, PTSD, drama triangles, narcissistic injuries, etc. We see ourselves as "sick" and unable to cure ourselves, so we internalize our pain, and then we are forced to self-medicate—mostly with the wrong substances or habits.

Having adopted many of these harmful habits, we are crippled by shame and guilt and have enormous difficulty admitting them to our families or close friends. This is true across the spectrum of Jewish communities regardless of origin, observance, or denomination. Families, both traditional and more secular, find it a failing of theirs to admit that their members, both children and adults, are battling addiction, mental illness, or lack of drive. The tyranny of the possible "*shanda*" (shame) hovers over many Jewish families and institutions. We fail to adopt inclusive practices that would invite the individuals and their families into public discourse and into our sacred spaces. Quite simply, we have chosen to present to the world a façade of the "good Jewish family" instead of addressing the needs of our community for inclusion. The old adage of "Jews don't drink/do drugs/go to prison/have AIDS," etc. not only has never been true; it negates the very essence of our tradition of caring for *all* and especially those who need help the most.

Spirituality, Not Just Religion

We confuse spirituality with religion. In today's world, for many, religion can be polarizing. For the believer, it is a place of great refuge and strength. For the nonbeliever it is a place where they are judged and live life through a prism that divides the world into a binary system—us/them, pure/impure, holy/secular, believer/infidel, etc. Still, many live somewhere along this spectrum. It is important to examine how we fit into the space between the polarities—a space that is ever-changing and ever-growing. We must approach spirituality through multiple pluralistic entry points.

We often forget that at the core of many religions lies a truth, a spiritual one—one that has been obscured by time and institution: our existence is determined by our God-given soul, a force that is strong and unique. It is what shapes our view of the world and how we choose to exist in it. Our soul, given to each of us, is the essence of our being—singular, designed to give each of us a particular nature or presence in this world, full of potential and limitless possibilities. As such, our soul is worthy all in itself. It is not just divine, but a reminder of our worthiness at any given moment. It is the force behind a lifelong journey, one that seeks to find meaning and understand our place in the world. This spiritual quest, which should be motivated by our questions and our intentions, can be part of our religion, but it does not have to be. Religion is an affiliation, an institution—something we belong to. Spirituality is the language we have for our experiences, insights, and truth gained from our journey.

The Role of Fear

We all experience fear, a feeling that stems from perceived danger or threat. In some cases, our lives might be threatened; but we also experience fear when we think that other people's views of us, or their treatment of us, is endangered. Fear is a powerful agent that can cause us to change our behavior, or causes us to run away, hide, or be paralyzed. It is the source of ignorance, hate, and marginalization of those who we think are not like us, or *other*. Fear is one of the root causes of non-inclusive practices and the enemy of pluralism.

Faith is a Practice

Believing, while often associated with religion, is really a daily human practice. We do it every day, but we lack the secular vocabulary to describe it. Faith is hope. Faith is love. Faith is the ability to allow something to pass because we assure ourselves that something else, something better, is coming—a different emotion or a different experience. Our perspective is enhanced by such faith. It's like having a much better vantage point, where we are given a chance to see beyond the moment and ourselves—and to think of the possibilities in our lives. Our actions, our emotions, and our journey are all part of our practice. Make your bed in the morning, start a fitness routine, change one thing about your day with the hope that it will improve you. The perspective we gain from this is immense, but we can only gain it if we shift our focus from our current experience and look at the bigger picture. Ask yourself: *How do I wish to be better? Can I see myself in a different situation? Can I be content with what I have? Do I have goals for the next week, month, year, three years? How do I achieve those goals?*

Doubt is a Value

While faith is the motor of well-being, as it helps us believe in a better tomorrow and the ability to transform ourselves and the world, too much hope can lead us to an unrealistic perspective—a kind of magical thinking. When faith becomes ardent, it closes the mind to possibilities. Doubt is the partner of faith, and for the seeker can be as comforting as faith. Doubt leads us to ask questions, think critically, and not accept the world as it is or our own shortcomings. Believing is the gas pedal and doubt is the brakes, helping us to go not too fast, not to overexert ourselves, not to cause harm when we take a turn too fast.

Today's world values certainty and clarity above all. One of the more difficult lessons about doubt is that it can lead to insecurity and anxiety. However, when paired with faith, doubt can be a powerful pillar of a happy, contented life.

Seeking the advice of others when working on an idea or a project and allowing your questions to inform their feedback is a practice of doubt. Just because you feel or think something does not mean that it's true. Accepting this is, in itself, an act of doubt. Allowing yourself to not accept everything as it is just because "that's how we always do it" is an act of doubt.

Doubt can be a catalyst to creativity and creation. Doubt causes us to stop and examine a situation, not taking for granted how the world presents itself. With doubt, we can see the world differently, the way we wish it would be. In a world that can be grand and divine, yet can present itself as harsh and cold, doubt allows us to pause and consider a different point of view. Helping us achieve ataraxy, doubt enables us to think of different possibilities and, by doing so, doubt allows us to tap into a sense of wonder and amazement.

Non-Binary Point of View

We need to move away from an either/or perspective toward a both/and perspective (I learned this and much more from Harriet Rossetto at Beit T'Shuvah in Los Angeles). As we grow and experience life, we learn. While the trajectory of our lives may not be linear and may take us off the path of wellness, we strive to be slightly better today than we were yesterday.

Following our tradition, we aim to learn from the past and use prior events as guides for our future. Feminism, social justice, LGBTQI+, and queer theory have moved us into the modern era with many insights and lessons, but none has been greater than a shift in our perspective on the spectrum of identity and a non-binary point of view.

While many would have us cling to a binary system that forces us to choose between good/bad, us/them, pure/impure, holy/secular, believer/infidel, male/female, gay/straight, our tradition teaches us that our *yetzer*—our creative, rejuvenating force—consists of two elements that create a spectrum: Good and what is often translated as "evil" (רע), but would be better translated as "other." This agathokakological reading teaches us that good and other exist within us, creating a tension. That tension demands us to hold both ends of the spectrum constantly, catering to our will to do and be good, and our inherent need to misbehave and create mischief. Negating either one of them leads to a life that is lacking, oppressive and unrealistic, leaving us hollow and in a constant state of misery.

We must shift our perspective from a binary either/or perspective to a both/and perspective, one that takes into consideration all our intentions, feelings, and actions. We should aim for a nuanced, complex existence—one that allows people to be who they are and not who we want them to be or expect them to be.

Immersive Torah

There are many Torah scholars: knowledgeable, articulate, clever people who know the story of the Jewish journey by heart. They can tell you where a random idea or quotation comes from, and easily navigate the sea of Talmud.

Content knowledge, the essential building block of Jewish life, is indeed a prized skill. As a child, in yeshiva, we would be quizzed every Friday on the weekly *parsha* (Torah portion). Endless questions involving a piece of a *pasuk* (a verse from the bible) asking us, "Who said this and to whom?" We were made to memorize unusual passages like the Song of the Sea and many others parts of Torah, Midrash, and Talmud.

However, knowing Torah is not enough, and perhaps even promotes a hierarchy for those who memorize better than others. But it fails to ask: How is knowing Torah and living Torah different? Knowing Torah is not enough to define us or give our lives meaning. Content may be an essential part of our religion and culture, but it does not promote living well. That part is up to us.

This is where living Torah comes in. It is easy to read our *parsha* and see the characters and events as foreign to us, to judge them, and not to see how their experience relates to our current lives. After all, we were not in Egypt, we did not see the miracles of the parting of the sea, or the pillars of smoke and fire. Surely, we would stand up and listen if God spoke to us, right? Or would we?

Content means little without meaning. Knowing things serves the ego and the constructed, self-important self; that part of us that we want to show to the external world: our role, our achievements, and our biography. It is necessary, but it is hollow unless you fill it with meaning. Knowledge without meaning is a façade concealing a void.

When we learn Torah, we must go beyond what we know to what we understand. This can be difficult because it requires us to leave what we can retell or repeat, and instead examine how we know what we know and how we see and experience ourselves in the text. We must expose our inner-self and learn how to relate to it. This can only happen through reading the text and bravely asking difficult questions.

What would happen if, indeed, one day you woke up and God spoke to you? Would you tell anyone? Who? Your doctor? Your partner? Your rabbi? Would you listen?

Freedom and Surrender

Have you ever asked yourself if you are truly free? Are you willing to entertain the idea that none of us are truly free? If so, how are you enslaved? To your job, to your addiction, to your money, to your fame?

Rabbi Mark Borovitz taught me many things (for which I am eternally grateful), but few as important as the idea that living Torah requires us to see ourselves in the story; it demands that we recognize that the people of Israel were human and that the human condition was as true, as sublime, and as painful for them as it is for us today. Without that recognition, our knowledge of their story becomes yet another piece of information that serves our constructed self. When we live Torah, we get to see ourselves. We identify not just the beautiful and heroic, but also the ugly and the despair in ourselves. That is a difficult task; one that not only demands that we see ourselves as a whole person, good and bad, but also that we face ourselves and the responsibility we have for our actions. We need to face our shame, guilt, and the rationalizations we tell ourselves when we choose to misbehave, as well as our positive urges that drive us to do good, to be of service, and to heed the advice of our elders. It is the essence of our surrender: an echo of an ancient and clear commandment.

The *Shema* prayer is not only the core of our liturgy but also a commandment to be still, to bow our head, to listen, and to choose to hold on to words and wisdom of our tradition, such that we are part of it and part of a larger whole. It is an acknowledgment that we uphold our part of the covenant with our community and with God, to hear, comply and execute our part in it. We strive not to succumb to fear, but to acquiesce to love and faith. By doing so we learn the value of surrender.

Complexity and Vicissitude

We all feel things, all the time. Often, we feel multiple emotions at once. When we feel love, we also feel fear of the potential loss of that love. When we feel scared and uncertain, we also feel exhilarated. When we feel loss, we also often feel relief. But our emotions can control us if we don't pay attention. We can become enslaved to them, thinking they own us. Taking actions based on these emotions, without learning how to observe them, wait for them to pass or deepen, usually produces impulsive, destructive behaviors that harm us.

Learning that emotions change and pass is a key understanding of recovery. When we feel in the doldrums, even when we think it will last forever, it will not. Just like happiness, it will also go away. When we feel lonely, sad, upset, or anxious, we need to take a moment to ask ourselves what we are feeling; name the emotions; play out what we want to do; and see if we can, or should, do that; imagine a different response that we would have taken in the past; let the feeling pass; or allow ourselves to lean into it more.

In the Talmud Bavli, Bava Metzia 32b, we read: "The Gemara suggests: Come and hear proof from a *baraita*: If one encounters a friend whose animal collapsed and it is necessary to unload its burden, and one also encounters an enemy who needs assistance to load a burden onto his animal, the *mitzvah* is to assist the enemy, in order to subjugate one's *yetzer*." We learn here of our need to deal with our feelings and not succumb to them; to understand why we might feel that a person is our enemy and to confront that feeling so that we may understand its complexity.

Learning how to do this is hard, but when we do, we regain control of ourselves. We can then make choices that will benefit us and support a life of meaning.

Gratitude

Happiness is not a place where you can go and stay forever. Happiness, like all emotions, is fleeting. Moments are to be treasured and appreciated. Counter to what most people think, one can choose to be happy—not all of a sudden and not immediately, but with practice, one can learn how to be happier. The key to happiness is gratitude.

In our tradition, we start our day as we open our eyes with the prayer of *Modeh Ani*, "I give thanks." The prayer prompts us to ask, what you are truly grateful for? Gratitude is an attitude. Can you shift your perspective to see something that is good about your day or your life today? Maybe a choice you made today that you didn't yesterday? Can you appreciate the ability to reflect? When we practice gratitude (not just saying "thank you" to multiple things, moments, and people), we learn to appreciate things that make us happy. We can go back to it as a beacon when we are feeling less-than. "Who is a rich person?" the *mishna* in Avot (4:1) asks. "The person who is happy with what they have."

Ritual

Most spiritual traditions put an emphasis on rituals: prayer, mediation, blessings, food rituals, waking up rituals, community rituals, gratitude rituals, and awareness rituals are part of these traditions. Torah and Talmud study, in particular, are a cornerstone of our tradition, an essential part of our identity, and key pillars of our recovery.

Ask happy/content and successful people about their daily lives, and you will find rituals—daily practices—such as making a bed in the morning, reading the newspaper with breakfast, doing a crossword puzzle on the way to work, or drinking a cup of tea before going to sleep. Rituals are milestones in our day. They primarily serve as a backdrop, a canvas on which we paint the details of our life. If we wake up at the same time every day, or take a walk at the same time and place, it helps us check in with ourselves and highlights how we feel. Do I feel different today? Why am I more tired, or more energized? What did I do different earlier?

Through rituals, we get to refine our reactions, our attitudes. Plan out our actions, creating (new) habits. If we choose to change something, it's only when we keep doing it over and over again that we are able to start acting differently, feeling differently, being differently. Going randomly to the gym won't change your habits or your body, but going regularly could. Not gossiping will not change how you feel about yourself immediately, but in time it will allow you to be more confident and self-assured. Knowing how we would feel after a walk on the beach, reading before going to bed, or journaling after dinner will help us to be more in control of ourselves and more in touch with our inner selves and what inspires us. Only daily practice and ritual can offer that.

Holiness

Being made in the image of God (*Imago Dei*) means that, from the moment we are born, we have divine intrinsic value. Everyone has a significant role to play in one's own life and the lives of others. Everyone has a value that is unique and unequivocal. It is when we lose sight of this that we cause harm to ourselves and to others. When we forget or choose to obscure this reality, we cause pain. Equally, when we isolate ourselves or drown our misery in drugs, alcohol, or other addictions, we lose connection to our intrinsic worth.

It is by accepting our own value that we can start our path in recovery. *Imitatio Dei*, Imitation of God, is the tool we use to bring greater value, holiness, and self-worth to our lives.

When we aspire to grow and better ourselves, we can choose to take on more godly virtues. Leviticus 19:2 states, "Speak to the entire assembly of Israel and say to them: 'Be holy because I, the Lord your God, am holy.'"

Our lives not only have value all on their own. When we choose to follow the path of holiness and compassion, we are beacons of hope and inspiration to others. The Talmud states: "As He is merciful, so should you be merciful" (Talmud Bavli, Shabbat 133b).

Study, Learn, Try New Things

It is somewhat paradoxical that many of us feel better when we challenge ourselves, when we engage with life trying to learn new skills (even, and perhaps especially, when we fail along the way). It is a basic tenet of our tradition that a person must make time to study and learn every day. Whether it is the minimum reading of two verses from the Torah and its translation to Aramaic (Unkelus), or a more complex ritual such as *daf yomi*, the learning of a page of Talmud per day, we must create space in our lives for growth, new perspective, debate, and understanding.

Learning a new skill, a new language, a craft or an art, or exploring new things, inspires us. It offers us a creative glimpse into possibilities that we did not think about before. (With a partner or a family member or a friend, learning new things together is a great way to strengthen your relationships, more so than showing the other person something that you already know and like.) Growth is an act of creation—of making new meaning in life. In a clear case of *Imitatio Dei*, we seek to create anew. Such is the inspiration for what comes from the beauty of learning and studying. Ask yourself, what is your favorite meal? Can you make it? What else would you like to try? Do you have a favorite poem? Can you memorize it?

When we connect with what inspires us, we are able to go back to that thing when we need to. A strong spiritual core depends on inspiration and a life of meaning is full of it.

No Person is an Island

When we isolate ourselves, we suffer. When we don't interact with others and sense our own humanity and theirs, we suffer. When we think we are alone and unappreciated, we suffer. When we don't feel that our existence matters to anyone, we suffer. Humans are social beings: we belong in communities, and when we acknowledge that, help others, and see their lives as they mirror ours, we thrive. The human condition is a condition we all have, and when we connect to this fact, we can grow.

Finding ways to be of service is a road to a happy, contented life. When we give from ourselves and are able to serve others, those who are in need, we are not just serving them but, in turn, serving ourselves. The feeling we get from connecting to our humanity is unmatched by any other experience. When we engage in service of others, we acknowledge our connectivity and our deep responsibility as a community and society. Helping those around us is not an act of altruism, but an enactment of our part. It is an acceptance of our responsibility to them and to ourselves. The Mishnah teaches us: "You are not expected to complete the task, but neither are you free to avoid it" (Avot 2:21).

While we may not always feel that our efforts will result in much meaning, we are obligated to continue to try to connect with and help those around us. Shifting from self-seeking to looking at our interwoven existence can only be achieved by finding ways to help our community, volunteering, helping, and giving. It is an essential building block in a life of meaning.

Action is Everything

Change is hard, very hard. We say we want it, but it's terribly hard work. Most of our habits formed for a reason. Almost all addictions start as a solution to a problem: that drink before the party to ease our social anxiety; that game with our friends or at the casino to experience that thrill; the pills to stay up those crucial nights studying, or at work. Habits form and, even though many times we say we want to change, it's hard to do since the habits serve a purpose, however misguided. Change only happens when awareness, or the will to do something different, is met with equal force with action (repeatedly; see ritual above).

Just being aware of the need to change is not enough; wanting it is not enough. We have to commit to repeating action. Contrary action. Choosing to do something differently this time. Positivity is enhanced when intention and action are aligned. When we do what we say, we will act how we intend, and we will be in control of our actions (we may not be able to control our emotions, but we can control our actions). When our intention and actions are not aligned, we create dishonesty and inauthenticity. Those are poisonous seeds that grow and affect us, and those around us, negatively.

Brokenness

We must acknowledge that we are not perfect, that we should not wish to be perfect. We must acknowledge that the gift of *t'shuvha* that we have been given means that we must be able to use it. In order to use it, we must recognize our failings and our wish to learn from them. By admitting our failings and our responsibility to amend them, we are creating space for ourselves, others, and our community. A healthy community requires not just an expansion of our understanding of inclusivity and what we find acceptable to talk about, but also contraction of ourselves to create more space for others around us.

This spiritual principle of *tzimtzum*, or reduction of self, places us at the center of a tense and complex spectrum of importance. Reb Bunim of Peshischa taught that a person must have two notes in his pockets. In one pocket should be a note that reads, "The world was created for me." In the other pocket, there should be a note that reads, "I am nothing but dust and ashes." The tension between these two is the constant pull between our self-important and self-protecting side and our self-effacing, honest, and critical side.

The traditional articulation of the Jewish way of life is *halakha*, deriving from the root *halakh* (הלכ), which means to walk. Shifting the tension from one side to another we move forward. Walking is nothing if not a controlled falling. This tension and forward momentum remind us that we are not one thing; we are not static. We are in constant tension, prepared to veer one way or the other as cracks appear on our path, but always moving forward.

When we are honest with ourselves, we realize that we are all broken, but it is through this brokenness that we can see each other's struggles. Only then can we connect and recover.

About the Contributors

Judith Aronson has been a Jewish Educator in both Massachusetts and California. She holds a Master of Theology degree from the Harvard Divinity School and is an alumna and fellow of Brandeis University. Her publications include "A Time for Living 1975: The Modern Jewish Family Calendar." An expert in mentoring, her article on that subject appears in *The Ultimate Jewish Teacher's Handbook*.

Rabbi Adam Chalom, Ph.D., is the Dean for North America of the International Institute for Secular Humanistic Judaism. He also serves as Rabbi of Kol Hadash Humanistic Congregation in north suburban Chicago, Illinois. He serves on the Executive Committee of the Association of Humanistic Rabbis and the Editorial Board of the journal *Humanistic Judaism*.

Rabbi Mordecai Finley, Ph.D., is Rabbi of Ohr HaTorah Synagogue, Los Angeles, and a Co-Founder of the Academy for Jewish Religion California, where he is Professor of Jewish Thought. He holds a Ph.D. in Religion and Social Ethics from the University of Southern California.

Dr. Tamar Frankiel is a retired Professor of Comparative Religion (Ph.D., University of Chicago) and former President and Provost of the Academy for Jewish Religion California. As provost, she helped to create a Christian-Jewish-Muslim-Buddhist network of seminaries and Jewish/Latter-day Saints Academic Dialogue, to which she still contributes. She is the author or co-author of eight books on Jewish spiritual practice and author of three books on the history of Christianity and American studies. She continues to lecture in Los Angeles, mentors dream groups, and writes both scholarly articles and fiction.

Cantor Jonathan L. Friedmann, Ph.D., is Professor of Jewish Music History and Associate Dean of the Master of Jewish Studies Program at the Academy for Jewish Religion California, President of the Western States Jewish History Association, Director of the Jewish Museum of the American West, and the author or editor of twenty-five books on Judaism, music, and religion. He also leads Adat Chaverim–Congregation for Humanistic Judaism, Los Angeles, and Bet Knesset Bamidbar, an unaffiliated Reform synagogue in Las Vegas.

Dr. Joel Gereboff is Associate Professor of Religious Studies at

Arizona State University and Professor of Bible and Jewish History at the Academy for Jewish Religion California. His research and publications focus on early rabbinic Judaism, American Judaism, Jewish ethics, and Judaism and the emotions.

Rabbi Mel Gottlieb, Ph.D., is President and Interim Dean of the Rabbinical School of the Academy for Jewish Religion California, where he also teaches courses in mysticism, biblical commentaries, and Hasidism. He has taught in various academic settings, including Columbia University School of Social Work, Yeshiva University, USC School of Social Work, and Pacifica Graduate Institute, and has served as Hillel Director at MIT and Princeton University, and as rabbi of several congregations in Los Angeles. Rabbi Gottlieb is involved in numerous interfaith and social action initiatives, and has published widely on topics ranging from spiritual psychology to ethical eating.

Rabbi Igaël "Iggy" Gurin-Malous is a spiritual counselor, artist, and educator. He is a frequent author, speaker, teacher and contributor on subjects ranging from Talmud, Jewish text, spirituality, addiction, recovery, fatherhood, and LGBTQI+ issues. He is the Founding Rabbi and CEO of T'shuvah Center, a new long-term Jewish recovery community in Bed-Stuy, Brooklyn.

Dr. Ora Horn Prouser is CEO, Academic Dean, and Professor of Bible at the Academy for Jewish Religion in Yonkers, New York. She has worked extensively on Bible pedagogy and is the author of many articles on biblical studies, specifically focusing on its intersection with gender studies, disability studies, and the arts. Her book, *Esau's Blessing: How the Bible Embraces Those with Special Needs*, was recognized as a 2012 National Jewish Book Council finalist and a Gold winner in the 2016 Special Needs Book Awards.

Rabbi Yocheved Mintz is Rabbi Emerita and Senior Educator for Congregation P'nai Tikvah, Las Vegas. A teacher and lecturer, she is Past President of the Board of Rabbis of Southern Nevada and of OHALAH, and is a member of the boards of Jewish Nevada, the Academy for Jewish Religion California, the Jewish Family Service Agency of Southern Nevada, and the Interfaith Council of Southern Nevada.

Cantor Lisa Peicott serves as Cantor at Wilshire Boulevard Temple in Los Angeles. She is a graduate of the Academy for Jewish Religion California, where she was ordained in 2018. Cantor Peicott resides in

Los Angeles with her husband, Joseph Peicott, and son, Joey.

Rabbi and Cantor Eva Robbins is Co-Spiritual Leader of Congregation N'vay Shalom, an independent facilitator of lifecycle ceremonies, and a teacher of Hebrew, *Tefillah* (prayer), and Torah. A graduate of the Academy for Jewish Religion California, where she is also on the faculty, Rabbi Eva is a fiber artist of Jewish ceremonial objects, the author of *Spiritual Surgery: A Journey of Healing Mind, Body, and Spirit*, and a guest columnist for the *Jewish Journal of Greater Los Angeles*. She is also a Reiki master and instructor of Jewish Meditation.

Rabbi Stephen Robbins, Psy.D., a graduate of Hebrew Union College, is a Co-Founder and Past-President of the Academy for Jewish Religion California, where he teaches mysticism, liturgy, and practical rabbinics. He is also Co-Founder and Co-Spiritual Leader of Congregation N'vay Shalom. Rabbi Robbins holds a Psy.D. from Ryokan College, has a Kabbalistic psycho-spiritual healing practice, and is a member of International Association for Near-Death Studies.

Rabbi Rochelle Robins, ACPE Certified Educator, is Vice President and Dean of the Chaplaincy School at the Academy for Jewish Religion California. She is also the Co-Founder and President of Ezzree.com, an online platform for chaplaincy and social services.

Cyd B. Weissman, M.Ed., M.A., is Vice President of Innovation and Impact at Reconstructing Judaism and on faculty at the Reconstructionist Rabbinical College in Wyncote, PA. She is the author of numerous articles on innovation and change in the Jewish community. Her Edge Blog (reconstructingjudaism.org/news/edgeblog) focuses on practical tools for shaping a better future in our changing times.

CPSIA information can be obtained
at www.ICGtesting.com
Printed in the USA
LVHW031137080221
678694LV00001B/83